Art in the Middle Ages

ART
in the
Middle
Ages

A Memoir
of Midlife Renaissance

Art Berman

BEAVER'S POND
PRESS

Art in the Middle Ages © 2023 by Art Berman

This book is memoir, and it reflects the author's memory of past events and conversations. Some names and identifying characteristics of people, places, and events have been changed to protect individuals' privacy.

Edited by Kerry Stapley
Book design and typesetting by Jim Handrigan
Author photo by Lauren Kiesel

ISBN 13: 978-1-64343-761-3
Library of Congress Catalog Number: 2022904077
Printed in the United States of America
First Edition: 2023
27 26 25 24 23   5 4 3 2 1

Beaver's Pond Press
939 West Seventh Street
Saint Paul, MN 55102
(952) 829-8818
www.BeaversPondPress.com

To order, visit www.artinthemiddleages.com.

Contact Art Berman at www.artinthemiddleages.com for speaking engagements and interviews.

For Kate

No great work of art is ever finished.
—Michelangelo

CONTENTS

PART I

The Downward Spiral

1

IS THIS REALLY HAPPENING?

Who will buy this wonderful morning?
Such a sky you never did see.
Who will tie it up in a ribbon,
And put it in a box for me?

—Lionel Bart, from the musical *Oliver*

7:30 a.m. It's a breathtakingly beautiful late-summer morning, one experienced maybe a half-dozen times a year. I lean forward, loosely gripping the commuter ferry's smooth upper-deck railing. I'm blissfully enveloped by a cool breeze. The boat's rhythm, as it gently rises and falls through the light surf, is hypnotic. I slowly inhale the saltwater-infused air; it's both calming and exhilarating. A graceful flock of seagulls, winging alongside us, complements the scene with a familiar cacophony. Eyes closing, I savor an exquisite moment and softly sing, "Who will buy this wonderful morning?"

I gradually open my eyes, serenely scan ahead, and take mental snapshots I will store forever. Juxtaposed against the cloudless eastern sky is lower Manhattan's larger-than-life skyline, casting long morning shadows. Its grandeur literally grows by the minute as we steam toward it. Looking south, there's the distant Verrazzano-Narrows Bridge, connecting Staten Island and Brooklyn. Its majestic expanse is set against the subtly graded, calming deep-blue horizon. My thoughts drift lazily to another evocative moment, thirty-six hours prior. I sat in Newark's minor league baseball stadium with my eight-year-old son, Max, and his best friend, Nick, enjoying a game on a balmy, starlit summer evening. It was a dream—so carefree and sweet—one of those lovely shared experiences between a father and son. It stirred decades-old memories of annual trips to Yankee Stadium with my own dad and brother. Those moments had been perfection, their warmth to be savored.

Life is good.

One hour later, I sit quietly at my desk, the morning's beauty faded from my consciousness. I mute my speakerphone, nervously check my to-do list, and half listen to the obligatory weekly conference call for American Express's international finance leadership team.

"And then we have to have consolidated numbers for Asia by Friday . . ."

Blah, blah, blah, I think. *This is such a waste of time.* Feeling stuck as the call drones on, I scan my monitor's newsfeed to pass the time. It's 8:45 a.m., and the date is September 11, 2001.

I see no news other than the usual stuff: reports of the latest economic data, market opening expectations, and new securities issuances. It's just another business day in lower Manhattan. My focus rapidly shifts to my immediate needs—how can I get off this call, get another cup of coffee, and get on with my day?

I am comfortably ensconced in my 29th floor office of American Express Tower, with a north-facing view of Midtown Manhattan. The World Trade Center complex, which is across the street to the east, is not visible from my office. This call will go on for a while. *Will anyone notice if I quickly sneak out for that cup of coffee? Probably not.* I can never get enough caffeine to start my day.

I'm about to get up, and I feel it—a very soft jolt. *Did the building just shudder?* I immediately sit up straight, senses on alert. If I hadn't experienced this before, I would think nothing of it. My mind goes straight back to 1993, when a massive bomb detonated in the World Trade Center's parking garage, killing eight people. I was walking down a nearby hallway when it struck. It was so strong that two colleagues walking toward me jumped and then dove, panicked, into an internal office doorway.

This jolt feels similar, but it is much fainter. I am not sure what just happened, though I know it was not normal. I stay on the call, wondering if any of the other New York–based participants felt anything. *Apparently not.* They continue to talk as if nothing happened. *Maybe it was nothing. Did I imagine it?*

I stand up and walk to my uptown-facing window, staring out and looking for a sign. I see nothing out of the ordinary. Satisfied and about to turn away, I then notice a few pedestrians are beginning to run. They keep turning around and pointing eastward.

My conference call just keeps going. "The card numbers are looking weak this quarter in Europe. We may need to reforecast the full-year outlook..."

I look at my newsfeed again, searching for some indication of what just happened. I don't know what to expect; it's only been a minute or two since I felt that soft shudder. Unsurprisingly, there's nothing. I am mystified.

Then I begin to hear the faint sound of distant sirens. The sirens grow stronger, becoming a relentless blare. *It was something—something is wrong.* I listen with growing worry and then decide to interrupt the conference call. "Something just happened," I say, directing my voice assertively toward my speakerphone. "You guys carry on, but I need to get off the phone right now." A colleague eleven floors above me is talking when I interrupt. He stops abruptly. There are a few seconds of awkward silence. I can tell that no one on the call has any clue why I interjected. I excuse myself and hang up. Weeks later, one call participant will tell me that after I got off, people openly wondered what possessed me to exit the call in such an uncharacteristic manner.

At that moment, a colleague breathlessly storms into my office. "Art, a plane just crashed into the North Tower!" We both jog down the hall to the east side of our building, the side that faces the World Trade Center. It stands just a few hundred feet away. Two dozen coworkers are congregated by the large bay of windows. We are all transfixed, staring across the street, looking straight up to the tower's top. There is a wall of black smoke billowing out across the full horizontal expanse of a high floor.

Having little comprehension of what just happened, we watch with a morbid curiosity, hoping that not too many people were hurt. There is even a bit of a blasé attitude among our rubbernecking crowd. One colleague reflects, "It was probably just some light aircraft pilot who fell asleep or had been drinking. It's too bad. I hope the fire department gets here soon so that they can take care of it."

Should I call Kate to tell her what's going on? At this moment, my wife, Kate, is in a parents' meeting at Max's elementary school. *No,* I think, *no need to alarm her unnecessarily.*

The clouds of black smoke are getting more and more dense, and our concerns grow. Still, there is absolutely no understanding of what happened or what is to come. Then someone yells, "Hey, there are people sitting on the window ledges!" We all strain to see them through the smoke. They are barely visible, but if we concentrate, we can see a dozen hazy figures. There are people dangling their legs over the edge. They appear to be looking down. It's a horrifying sight—the first of many that day—and one that will forever haunt me.

Oh my God, when will the fire department get here? We all have other urgent, private thoughts. *Who do I know who works in the North Tower?* We all know someone. *What firms are based on the top floors? Who do I know at Cantor, Fitzgerald? Deloitte? Isn't there an American Express office up there? Yes! What departments?* Our collective anxiety for those poor souls across the street feverishly grows.

Our head of operations briskly walks the halls and provides assurances. "Don't worry. Stay in place. There's no need to evacuate. We've been told that it's under control. The police and fire departments are on the scene. It's under control."

Our office building's security team provides similar calming assurances over our public address system. "A small plane struck the

North Tower of the World Trade Center. The New York City Fire and Police Departments are on the scene and are handling it. We are safe in our building. There is no need for us to evacuate. We will keep you apprised of any further developments." That was the last time we heard from building security.

I am scheduled for another conference call at 9:00 a.m., this one for the leadership team of my business unit, American Express's international banking subsidiary (American Express Bank, or "the Bank"), where I am chief financial officer and treasurer. The New York–based team meets in a windowless conference room, and our Bank colleagues from Europe and Asia call in. As the meeting starts, we share theories about what is happening. We then receive more shocking news—another plane just struck the South Tower of the World Trade Center. This puts us over the edge. *What the hell is going on?* We are the next tallest building in the area. *Could we be the next target?*

We all feel imminent danger. Our CEO coolly and urgently says, "Let's stay calm. Round up your staffs. We need to evacuate right now." When I go to look for my finance team, I am glad to see that most are already gone. I walk over to our trading room where I have other staff members who are responsible for trading securities and money market products. Everyone is calmly transferring key financial transaction information to our London-based team before exiting the building. This is just in case we can't get back into the office until tomorrow.

I speak to my colleague, Victor, who supervises the trading room, about what we need to do. I am impressed by his business-like demeanor in sorting things out. He assures me that everyone will depart within five minutes. I thank him and leave in order to do one last walk around the floor. Little could we have imagined that within ninety minutes, this part of the building will not exist except as street-level rubble; it will be sheared off when the North Tower collapses, and it will be a year before we can return.

Satisfied that all my staff left, I head for the exit. The stairway swells with more and more people as we reach the lower floors. We all move along urgently but without panic. Finally exiting the building, the first thing I see is chilling. There are misshapen metal parts of an airplane, none more than a few feet long, littering the ground right outside our front door. I carefully step around them.

Not sure what to do or where to go, I head for my usual form of transportation out of New York City, the New Jersey ferry. It is just a few minutes' walk from my office. As I approach the small ferry terminal, the crowd is dense and rapidly growing. It is immediately clear that few will be able to board the one available boat.

I think that perhaps I should stick around. Just maybe I will be able to go back to work once the fire department gets the situation under control. It did not occur to me to grab my laptop on my way out of the office, or even to turn off my desktop computer. It's hard to fathom in retrospect, but when I left the building, I expected to return that day.

As the air fills with black smoke rising from the two towers, the situation's gravity continues to sink in. My thoughts of returning do not last long. Hundreds of us stand still and watch, mesmerized by the sight of thick, puffy black smoke coming from the two buildings. The lower Manhattan sky darkens, and an acrid smell fills our nostrils. The crowd slowly but viscerally becomes gripped by fear.

We look around at each other and start asking questions, strangers freely engaging strangers.

"What are you going to do?"

"What are our options?"

"The subways are probably not running."

"What *can* we do?"

There are few choices, and it is increasingly clear that staying is the worst among them. I slowly pick my way through the crowds, now determined to leave the area. Walking up West Street along the Hudson River, I pull out my cell phone, finally having a minute to call Kate. My phone screen is blank; cellular service is dead.

I briskly head uptown along with a growing army of lower Manhattan office workers. Everyone keeps turning and looking downtown at the burning towers. We cannot believe what we are seeing. The tops of both towers are enveloped in black smoke. At 9:30 in the morning, on a beautiful day with sunshine in three directions, the sky above lower Manhattan is dark as night. It's shocking. It's incomprehensible. *Is this really happening?*

We are hungry for news, but we have very limited ability to access information. Continuing the trek uptown, people congregate by the dozens around convertible cars whose blaring radios provide the only reliable news source. Joining one of the crowds and straining to hear, I listen to reports of two planes striking New York City, and a similar attack on the Pentagon. I am bewildered. (The fourth plane, which crashed in Pennsylvania, is not yet being reported.)

I try to think rationally about what to do. My most urgent concern, in addition to moving away from downtown, is to somehow contact Kate and let her know that I am okay. Although cell phones are not working, there are still plenty of landline pay phones along Manhattan's streets. With each street-side pay phone I pass, I do a quick calculation—is it worth waiting in lines fifteen to twenty people deep, or should I keep walking? At first it's an easy decision, and I keep moving in search of a shorter line. As I progress up West Street, I realize that the lines aren't getting any shorter; they are getting longer. Some people get creative. They give others at the front of the lines their personal information and their loved ones' telephone numbers, asking that this information be passed along, and that an additional call be placed on their behalf. I am not going to do that. I want to speak directly to Kate, so I keep walking.

There are many surreal sights and sounds along the way. Hundreds of ambulances are lined up quietly on West Street. They are ready to spring into action once called, but there is no place for them to go and nothing yet for them to do. They all sit idly, and they will remain unmoving all day. The ambient noise, however, is deafening, and it will stay that way for hours. The piercing sound of other sirens passing nearby is unrelenting.

Scores of low-flying helicopters create a frequent, irregular buzzing sound. Every time a helicopter flies over, everyone looks up and instinctively ducks in fear, wondering whether or not a third airborne missile is about to strike.

Thousands of people line up at piers that run all the way up the Hudson River, hoping to catch a ride on any boat, most of them privately owned, out of Manhattan. Besides walking, this is one of the few ways one can get out of the city today.

There are dozens of random joggers. People are jogging in the middle of all this! They, like the rest of us, move along with their eyes glued to what is happening downtown.

Early on in my march uptown, someone yells, "Gas leak!" Total panic ensues. With visions of a fireball racing up West Street, everyone starts running and screaming until they are out of breath. Then we continue our northward trek more slowly, our backs to the horror.

At one point those looking back start screaming again. I turn around as the South Tower begins to fall. About a mile away, it is clearly visible. The tower descends straight down in what appears to be slow motion, raising a monstrous cloud of billowing dust. I can only hear the relentless noise of everything around me, not the sound of a collapsing building. Later accounts of the tower's collapse from nearby witnesses will describe it as sounding like an earsplitting, rumbling train. I can see, but cannot hear, as the tower silently slips out of sight, replaced only by a mushrooming dust cloud.

I pick up my pace. I am still trying to comprehend the gravity of these events; how stunningly, unexpectedly, and completely life is changing; and how it is happening in the moment.

Is this really happening? A little over two hours ago, cast against a storybook late-summer daybreak, I marveled at lower Manhattan's beautiful skyline from my ferry's deck. I smugly observed how good I had it while softly singing "Who Will Buy This Wonderful Morning?" My mind is spinning madly.

I try to focus on the immediate task of finding a phone. I turn eastward and walk into Greenwich Village. I'm hopeful that if I get away from the river it will be less congested and the payphone lines will be shorter. Sure enough, after walking several blocks, the crowds thin. There's a phone where only a few people are waiting, and I take my place in line.

Impatiently waiting my turn, I am able to see the North Tower.

It is now standing alone against the dark lower Manhattan sky. After ten minutes, I make the call and reach Kate.

"It's me!" I shout into the phone. The ambient noise is still deafening.

"Oh my God!" she cries, and she starts sobbing.

"It's okay! It's okay! I'm okay!"

"Thank God!" she replies, taking a few moments to gather herself. "I'm so relieved! Where are you?" she urgently asks.

"I'm in the Village. I'm fine."

"Get away from downtown, Art! Get away! It's too dangerous there! And stay away from Times Square too! We don't know what's going on or what could happen next!"

The news reports she shares are dire, and we don't know what to think. We quickly cycle through names of friends who also work downtown, wondering aloud about their offices' proximity to the World Trade Center and how they might be doing.

She describes what happened at the school parents' meeting that morning, how she couldn't understand why people kept leaving the room to take calls, never coming back. As the news broke, the meeting quickly ended and all the parents went home. Meanwhile, school administrators decided to keep school in session to maintain as much normalcy as possible for the children.

This is an especially traumatic event for our New Jersey town (and dozens of others in the immediate area), as a high proportion of town residents work in lower Manhattan. More than a dozen town residents will die today, including three parents of children at Max's school.

While talking to Kate, I keep staring downtown at the North Tower, trying to comprehend the sight of a single tower now occupying space where, for the last thirty years, twin towers had stood. While still on the phone and entertaining that very thought, the North Tower collapses. It looks the same as when the South Tower fell—a slow-motion dropping into a mushrooming cloud of dust. It feels like the world is coming to an end.

"Art, come home! Just get out of there!"

"Okay, okay! I will get home as soon as I can. I'm trying to figure out how to get out of New York. I don't think that public transportation is running."

The day's glorious weather adds to its surreal quality. West Village restaurants are open for business, and many provide outdoor seating. They all offer free food, drinks, and a friendly respite for shell-shocked residents and wandering commuters like myself. These are kind gestures, and merely the first of many that I receive from strangers on 9/11. I take some water and then head back to West Street's riverfront to resume my walk uptown.

I figure that the only way out of town, at least to New Jersey, is by boat. People are patiently waiting in long lines for boats all along the riverfront piers. I don't have the patience, and I opt to keep on walking, hoping that by going uptown I will find shorter lines.

By the time I hit the west-Midtown area, it is midday, and I am ready for another break. I still don't want to wait in line, so I try to find lunch somewhere, hoping I'll come back to shorter lines later. I head east and find a convenience store, a restroom, an available pay phone, and a cool place to sit that is out of the sun. It's a welcome break. With cell phones still inoperable, I use the pay phone to call a few overseas work colleagues, leaving lengthy voicemails. They doubtlessly know about the attacks already, but I also want to tell them that to the best of my knowledge, we are all okay.

I return to the riverfront and am frustrated to find that the boat lines are even longer, each stretching many city blocks. It's time for patience. I pick a line and settle in for a few hours' wait, chatting with others as we share experiences. We have few facts, and we are all hungry for information. We know little except that we are witnesses and bit players in an extraordinary historic event.

I finally board a large ferry bound for Weehawken, New Jersey, in late afternoon. As we pull away from the dock and start across the river, it is so crowded that virtually all of us are standing shoulder-to-shoulder. I am on the upper deck, and as I stare back, I can also see the throngs of people on the lower deck. Everyone is spellbound, looking silently toward lower Manhattan. It is draped in a deathly shroud of black dust and enveloped from above by a dark gray cloud. There are hundreds of us, maybe more, and no one is speaking. Not a single person. We all watch in disbelief, lost in our own thoughts.

We disembark in Weehawken, a place I have never been, but one I will become very familiar with in the coming months. New Jersey Transit is offering bus rides to Hoboken, one town south, which has trains to our home in Chatham Township. I board a bus, we pull away, and within a minute we stop. The roads are so clogged we cannot move. I get off and end up walking to Hoboken. In total, I will walk over fifteen miles this day.

I make one stop on the way. I receive a message to participate in a 5:00 p.m. conference call of American Express's finance leadership team. I don't even remember how I got that message—I think it was on my Blackberry, or maybe Kate told me. As I approach the Hoboken train station on foot, I find an available pay phone on Washington Street, Hoboken's main commercial avenue. I am on the call for two hours, mostly listening. Call participants recount their own personal stories while also sharing information on their staff members. They discuss what, from a business perspective, they will do going forward. One thing is certain; we aren't showing up at the office tomorrow. I strain the entire time, trying to hear what is being said. There is a nonstop parade of emergency vehicles whizzing by, sirens blaring, up and down this busy thoroughfare. When it is my turn to talk, I practically shout into the phone. I can't imagine what the others on the call are thinking, especially the international participants.

I finally catch a local train and head home, arriving in Chatham around 10:00 p.m. As I exit the station to find my car, I have another heart-stopping moment. I had come home this late from work many times, and at this hour there were never more than five or six cars still in the parking lot. Tonight there must be fifty cars here. This sight shocks and sickens me. Anxiously searching for cars whose owners I know, I hope I won't find any. Thankfully, I don't.

I arrive home five minutes later. Kate will subsequently describe me as "shell-shocked and in a state of high alert." I am wired. We hug for a long time, not saying a word. Kate is sobbing, and I can feel my own tension drain away. Eight-year-old Max and two-year-old Elena are still awake and look on curiously.

"I am so relieved that you're home," Kate quietly says, still a little weepy. After our first morning call, I had checked in several times during the day, assuring her that I was okay, that I would be home as soon as possible, and to get the latest news updates.

"Who have we heard from?" We again cycle through names of friends who work downtown. A few are still not accounted for. We have very little information.

"What are we going to do now?" she asks.

"The first thing I need to do is to call everyone on my team and make sure they got home safely. After that, I have no idea."

This is a story about navigating my mid-life, roughly between the ages of forty-five and sixty: processing the impact of a life-changing, traumatic event; experiencing a career crash; reflecting on how I got there and how I might find my way out; and navigating an unexpected and transformative journey to renewal. This is my story.

2

THE MORNING AFTER

Let it be said
while in the midst of horror
we fed on beauty—and that,
my love, is what sustained us.

—Rita Dove, "Transit"

In 9/11's immediate aftermath, we all share a common question: *Did this really happen?* There is total disbelief. The event and the emotions are just starting to sink in, and they are unthinkable. *Did we imagine it? Could it possibly be just a bad dream?*

We are in uncharted territory—emotionally, personally, professionally, how we think about and plan our futures—pretty much in every meaningful way. Our New Jersey community and the greater New York City area are gripped by grief, fear, and anger.

Initially we focus on addressing the most urgent traumas—helping our friends and neighbors who lost family members. Kate immediately steps up as a strong community leader and advocate. She organizes parents and administrators at Max's school to provide day-to-day support, such as meals and family grief counseling. She also takes the lead in "adopting" one local family in particular. The mom is British, and she has a young son whose name, coincidentally, is Max. Her American husband worked in the World Trade Center and died on 9/11. We have them over for dinner, and she tells us that because she is not an American citizen and her husband is no longer living, she is being threatened with deportation. It's appalling, but it is the tenor of this period when our federal government views many foreign nationals with suspicion. Kate goes to work on her behalf, reaching out directly to New Jersey's U.S. senators. She successfully lobbies for their intervention and support so that our friend, and others in her position, will be allowed to remain in the country.

Professionally, I feel like I am plunging into the world of the completely bizarre. When I left my office the morning of 9/11, I left everything behind, assuming that I would be going back. As it turns out, I never physically returned to that office. It would take nearly a year to repair the building's damage sufficiently enough to allow for returning workers. After seventeen years of working at American Express in lower Manhattan, 9/11 would be the last day I'd ever work in New York City.

Kate and I are in the process of converting our home office into a nursery. She is three months pregnant with Elizabeth, our third child. The nursery is where I am setting up shop for a couple of weeks. I use our old HP desktop computer and rely on an AOL dial-up modem to access the internet.

In my leadership role at American Express's international bank subsidiary, I have unthinkable challenges when I wake up on September 12. Most poignantly, I have to physically account for all of my New York–based staff. Within a couple of days, I reconnect with all but one person, Carol.

No one knows Carol's whereabouts or if she is even alive. Phone messages go unreturned, and now her voicemail box is full. I keep trying anyway. It is unlike her to stay disconnected. I fear the worst, while urgently trying to conjure up a hopeful scenario.

A week passes by, and I am losing hope. Then my phone lights up with her caller ID.

"Carol?" I cry.

"Art?"

"Carol? Oh my God! It's such a relief to hear your voice!" I am practically shouting, and I quickly choke up. "We were worried sick about you. Where are you? Are you okay?"

"It's so good to hear your voice too, Art." She is calm, and I can hear the smile in her voice. "Yes, I'm fine. I'm at my mother's house in Cincinnati."

"What? Cincinnati? What are you doing there? We were so worried about you! I am so relieved to hear from you. Tell me how you're doing," I implore as rapid-fire thoughts come tumbling out.

"Art, I had a really bad experience on 9/11," she shares, her voice remaining calm, but now taking on a serious tone. "I'm still totally freaked out."

"What happened?" I ask, settling down. I brace myself. I had already heard a number of personal horror stories.

"I was walking to work that morning and was just a couple blocks away when the second plane crashed into the South Tower. It came out of nowhere. I . . . I don't really want to talk about it." She pauses and stops. I wait patiently and then realize that she is not going to continue.

"Oh my God! I'm so sorry, Carol." I process this information, imagining what she may have experienced, before continuing. "How are you doing now?"

"I'm better. But after that I turned around, walked back to my apartment, packed, got into my car, and left New York City. I don't really remember details. I just drove straight through to Ohio without stopping. I had to get out of there. I'm so glad to be out of there and to be home. I feel so much safer. I don't think I can ever go back to New York."

"I'm just so glad you're safe, Carol. I am so sorry for all of your trauma." Another pause, as I search for what to say next.

"I know, thanks Art," she quietly continues. "I'm going to hang out here for a while and then try to figure out what I'll do next. I can work from home, but I know I can't come back."

"I understand, Carol. You have to take care of yourself. We're all trying to process this. We're all traumatized."

We continue on. I update her on other work colleagues, and we do a little shop talk before wrapping up. We agree to stay in close contact.

Three months later, Carol moved back to New York City, and we welcomed her to work in our temporary New Jersey office. She would stay for a year before permanently relocating back to Ohio.

As I am accounting for all of my staff's whereabouts, I also have a doozy of a work-related headache. We literally cannot find $1 billion that had been in our bank accounts but magically disappeared from the Bank's records on 9/11. Our clearing bank was so seriously damaged on 9/11 that their records were destroyed, and their backup systems appeared to be permanently damaged. This blew my mind. How can $1 billion just disappear like that? And no one is stepping up to say, "Oops, our problem, we'll take care of it," or "here's a short-term loan so that you can pay your bills until we figure this out." Our bank's equity, at around $800 million, is less than the funds we just lost. I desperately try to wrap my brain around the implications and how to recover. There is no roadmap for dealing with this, nor is it a scenario that I ever imagined. It's a nightmare.

Our treasury team connects right away by phone, and we go to work. We have staff in New York as well as other money center locations—Singapore, London, Frankfurt—and within a couple of days, we successfully raise $1 billion and plug our short-term hole. At least for now, we will be able to pay our bills. Meanwhile, we problem-solve the larger issues to recover our funds. That takes a couple more weeks, and it all works out. Not that I ever had doubts, but I will never need another example of why teamwork, relationships, and trust matter. Exceptional teamwork is a recurring theme during this highly unusual period.

The next business task is to reconstruct our bank's budget and financial forecast. We have no access to our electronic or physical files, so we do this from memory while working from our homes. I have a separate team for this task, and we have daily calls to put the pieces together. We all create makeshift work arrangements from our homes as we face the logistical questions of how and where to reassemble. We want to regain a semblance of normalcy.

Our next step is to get together in New York City for a meeting with our external auditors, and then for a company-wide event at

Madison Square Garden. This is one week after 9/11, and it will be my first time back in the city. As I leave Penn Station that morning, the station's walls, now plastered with handwritten notices, are a raw, emotional reminder of our collective trauma. There are hundreds of notes randomly taped to the walls. They all have photographs, accompanied by descriptions and desperate, pleading messages. These are a common sight around New York City in the post-9/11 days.

"Have you seen my daughter? Son? Wife? Husband?" I cannot help but stop and read many of them. They're riveting and heartbreaking, and it is overwhelming to try to process this event's sweeping personal impact. It is also a heart-wrenching reminder of a tragic peculiarity—people who died, many of whom just happened to be proximate to the World Trade Center, simply did not return home that night. There is no other indication, such as physical evidence (at this stage), that can provide confirmation of their deaths. Nearly three thousand people are just missing and presumed dead. Still, one week later, families hold out desperate hope.

As I walk up Eighth Avenue, I approach a firehouse and involuntarily freeze. The two door bays are open, and there is a long table along the far wall with hundreds of lit candles. Above the candles are the pictures of fifty firefighters, formerly stationed at this firehouse, who perished. The bravery of these public servants humbles and awes me. These are men and women who rushed into burning buildings and slogged up dozens of flights of stairs, carrying fifty-plus pounds of weight, in a vain attempt to save hundreds of people. It was all for naught.

As I continue to stare, I see two firemen quietly talking to each other. They see me looking in. They solemnly nod in acknowledgment. I do the same, not knowing what to say or do. I then turn and continue walking.

Prior to the company-wide meeting, I host lunch for my New York–based staff at a nearby restaurant. It's the first time we are together since 9/11. I had to plead with a few of them to even attend, so fearful was the prospect of coming back into Manhattan. We all hug and share stories, and I do a lot of listening. I learn that several company employees who worked in the North Tower died, and that one colleague who was walking outside when the plane struck has life-threatening injuries caused by falling aircraft debris.

In the post-9/11 period, I experience New York City in a very different way. New Yorkers show strength and resilience, combined with extraordinary kindness. This inspires me and leaves an indelible impression. Living through this period cements an enduring love for this city and its people.

We work out of our homes for three weeks. The Bank's entire staff then reassembles at a temporary office in Weehawken, New Jersey. It feels odd that Weehawken, a place I first experienced by accident on 9/11, is now my temporary work home, and will be for a year in 9/11's immediate aftermath. For history enthusiasts, Weehawken is best known as the site of Aaron Burr's and Alexander Hamilton's famous duel in 1804, on the dramatic palisades just above the Hudson River.

To the contemporary local commuter, Weehawken is the access point for the New York City–bound Lincoln Tunnel. If someone on the Jersey side of the river descends the famous circular "helix" into the tunnel, they'll pass a massive billboard mounted on a squat, nondescript office building. That is the very building to which my team was relocated.

Working here answers two questions that I had occasionally considered on my many drives past: *Do people really work in that place? And is it possible to actually get there by car?* I never imagined that someday I would work there.

Our business unit occupies one large space with an open floor plan. The Bank's president and CEO, my boss, is the only person who gets an office, and there is one small meeting room to serve two hundred temporarily displaced workers. The rest of us have cubicles, and most of the professional staff double up in shared cubicles. I conduct private meetings, including staff performance reviews, in the stairwell.

Our midday meal options are severely limited. If you don't want to go outside and drive or walk quite a distance to eat, your only choice is the hallway food cart. It is run by the irrepressible "sandwich lady." She is short and stout, with frizzy brown hair, a cheerful disposition, and a smile that won't quit. If you close your eyes and just listen to her talk, you will swear you are talking to Carmela Soprano from the legendary HBO television show *The Sopranos*. Her heavy New Jersey accent totally charms me.

When we're hungry and tired of the food cart, we take our chances going out. There is only one (barely) viable choice of where to go. It is a bland office and hotel development down by the Hudson River. It has a couple of sit-down restaurants, a Sheraton hotel, and a food court for the area's office workers. There is just one problem—it is a very long walk, and nobody wants to get in a car and drive for lunch; we are, after all, New Yorkers. It is very close as the crow flies, but there are train tracks in between, and a tall chain-link fence stands between our building and the tracks.

Then, one day, I make a great discovery: there is a massive hole in the fence, and if you duck down a little, you can walk through and cross the tracks. It is one of my better contributions to our team, as I feel like I am liberating two hundred people to exercise freedom of food choice. But it does not make me popular with the sandwich lady, and I feel bad about that.

We have some adventurous outings through the chain-link fence. We learn not to go if it hasn't rained recently. I make that mistake once and find the path on the other side of the fence is so dry that my shoes and lower pant legs become completely dust-covered. We also learn to dodge the heavy freight train traffic. Often, one of my coworkers will shout "Let's run for it!" before a train passes; if we don't, lunch will be delayed by ten minutes. It is quite a sight—an out-of-shape set of middle-aged professional people sprinting across the tracks in front of an oncoming train. Many a lunch group is split up because some members make it across while others get stuck on the wrong side of the tracks.

Every "let's have lunch out" conversation starts with the question, "Shall we take the long way or go through the hole in the fence?"

The answer is usually to take the hole in the fence. When our entire team finally moves back to the company's New York City headquarters, one of our creative colleagues will make a large commemorative poster for all of the Weehawken-based staff. It will have three blown-up pictures on it: the New York City skyline as seen from Weehawken, the Weehawken entrance to the Lincoln Tunnel, and the iconic hole in the fence. I still have that poster.

The year I worked in Weehawken was, from a work-relationship perspective, my best ever. Among my colleagues, there was a strong sentiment of being in something together, an instinctive sense of a close-knit team's shared sacrifice. There were the challenges of supporting each other through post-9/11 personal traumas, as well as the camaraderie created by working in close quarters, helping each other through anxieties and frustrations, and being in such an idiosyncratic place as Weehawken. But while we built strong relationships and formed warm personal memories, there was also a deep and persistent sadness. We were always painfully aware of why we were there. My colleagues felt relieved and thankful to move back to New York City in the fall of 2002, more than a year after the 9/11 attacks. I, however, never moved back.

3

THIS IS MINNESOTA?

Only those who will risk going too far can
possibly find out how far one can go.
—T.S. Eliot

Following 9/11, American Express's businesses suffer terribly as the economy, already headed toward recession, takes a further nosedive. Investment plans are suspended and pessimism reigns as hopes are replaced by deep concerns. All of our business lines are stressed, and the company devolves to a scrambling mode.

American Express Financial Advisors, our Minneapolis-based asset management, insurance, and financial planning subsidiary, is particularly vulnerable due to weak financial markets. In an attempt to make up for lost earnings, Financial Advisors adopts an ill-conceived, highly risky investment strategy. It promptly implodes, creating a $1 billion loss in the second quarter of 2002. American Express's leadership is mercilessly skewered in the national media. The company looks inept, and the public embarrassment horrifies senior company leaders and major shareholders.

The inevitable management shake-up is swift, and there are several high-level departures. A new executive team, with power notably shifted toward New York–based leaders, is formed. Its task is to clean up the investment portfolio and to put the business on a more sustainable path. While I am not part of that team, I am aware of its work. I remain ensconced at the Bank subsidiary, our quirky Wee-hawken locale, and am content to deal with our own set of eclectic struggling businesses. It's a good time to stay under the radar.

With the embarrassing press coverage, leadership turnover, and confounding business challenges, it's a tough work environment at the Minneapolis-based subsidiary. This is particularly true in its finance department, where the chief financial officer (CFO) position sits vacant, the department is under intense pressure, and morale is generally viewed to be pretty awful.

Throughout the spring and summer of 2002, American Express conducts an external search to fill the Financial Advisors' open CFO position. It's a big job, and it turns up nobody—at least nobody who wants it. Financial Advisors has a New York–based interim CFO, Bob, and he agrees to stay until the permanent position is filled.

Finally, likely out of exasperation, company leaders look inside American Express for candidates to fill the open position. This is when I get a call from American Express's CFO.

I am gazing out of Greg's oversized, sun-drenched fiftieth-floor corner-conference-room window, waiting for him to arrive. Greg, as the company's CFO, was one of the first executives to move back into our lower Manhattan headquarters after 9/11. I am still working out of Weehawken, making this meeting my first trip back to the home office in ten months.

It feels like it happened yesterday. I am lost in thought. I grip the back of a chair and gently lean forward to steady myself as my muscles involuntarily tighten. The uninterrupted views from the tower's northeast corner, home to American Express's executive suite, are stunning—sweeping north to the Midtown skyline, and then east, to where the financial district's nearby skyscrapers punctuate the skyline like staccato notes hovering well above the staff.

It's a magnificent sight, yet its grandeur barely registers. I am morbidly fascinated by the scene below—the mundane, ground-level cityscape immediately across the street. I try to imagine the World

Trade Center's imposing North Tower that used to sit right there, almost as if you could reach out and touch it. But what I actually see is a massive, drab, rectangular, slightly depressed, and yawningly open dirt patch that covers several acres of what used to be the entire World Trade Center complex. It is a warren of activity. Dozens of tiny tractors and hundreds of workers move busily around the dirty space as if it is an ant colony.

"Good afternoon, Art," Greg perkily greets me as he bounces into the room. I immediately snap out of my midday reverie, spin around, and smile, and we share a warm handshake. In his late forties and prematurely gray, he has a compact frame, a studious look, a ready smile, and positive physical energy. He radiates warmth.

Greg is the consummate corporate professional—a sharp thinker, a highly polished communicator, a thoughtful leader, and a skilled internal politician. He has all the right credentials—Ivy League MBA, top-notch consulting firm experience, and CFO at other large companies from an early age. As a corporate animal, he is at the top of the food chain, and his impact at the company has been positive. He's earned respect from external investors, while also being a savvy internal organizational leader. I admire him, though his salesy style can sometimes put me off. We do not know each other well. I have always been two levels down from him, but we have a cordial and mutually respectful relationship.

We make small talk for a minute or two, and then he gets right down to business. Greg is not a small-talk kind of guy, at least not with me.

"Art, I'd like you to take the senior finance role in Minneapolis. You've done well as the Bank's CFO, and now I think it's time for you to take a bigger role."

"Thank you, Greg. I appreciate that vote of confidence." A colleague has given me a heads-up to expect an offer, and I don't miss a beat. But while responding, I also rapidly process his words, and I'm a little confused. Greg is a precise communicator. I think we are here to talk about the Financial Advisors' CFO position, but that's not what he said.

"Could you tell me more about the job?" I continue.

"Yes, this is the Senior Vice President job for Financial Advisors' Finance." Translation: *No, this is not the CFO job.* If it was, he would have said it.

What's he talking about?

I don't say a word, but my puzzled expression tells him what he needs to know.

"Well, my plan is a little complicated. I'm going to create a new job for you, Art. Financial Advisors is in a massive transition right now, and it's not clear how it will turn out. Bob came out of retirement, and he's leading that effort on my behalf. I need for him to continue as my interim CFO for Financial Advisors. He'll work out of New York, just like he is now, and you'll relocate and support the business on the ground in Minneapolis. I need you there. The place is in transition, and we have a lot of issues that require a strong leadership presence. Bob is going to work on the big-picture items from New York, like sorting out our investment portfolio and restructuring the businesses. I need you to work with the team on the ground, learn the business, and especially, help build a healthier work culture. In a year, we'll be through this transition. Assuming all goes according to plan, Bob will step down from his interim role and retire, and you'll get another promotion to CFO. By then, we'll be in an even better place."

Translation: *This is not the CFO offer that you may have been expecting. We'll talk about that next year after we see how things go. For now, I'll keep Bob here to do the big stuff, and I'll have you in Minneapolis to handle the sticky staff situation out there.* While I appreciate being asked, I'm not sure I like the sound of this two-step plan.

"Who will I be reporting to? Will I be reporting to you?" Even though I think I know the answer, I have to hear his words and reasoning.

Greg looks at me for just a moment, pausing before answering. He knows where I am going with this question. "No, you'll report to Bob. Then, when you get promoted to CFO, you'll report to me."

This is the answer I expected, but not the one I was hoping for. Bob was brought back to fix the horrendous portfolio problems at Financial Advisors. He is an accomplished financial strategist and is also known for his wit and wicked sense of humor. He's a good choice for fixing the problems. He's also a tough guy to work for.

Greg senses my discomfort, and he skillfully pivots to a selling mode. "I have to tell you, Art. I've only worked with Bob for three months, and he has been an absolute delight. He's smart, charming, and one of the funniest people I've ever met. The best part is he's getting so much done at Financial Advisors; I think we all could learn a lot from Bob." He stops there and looks at me for a reaction, seemingly satisfied that he addressed my concerns.

We hold eye contact, and I slowly nod. Every word Greg said about Bob is true. We both know that. We also know he painted an incomplete picture. No doubt my body language is still communicating some unease.

"I hear from Bob that you and he have a long and very good working relationship, Art," Greg continues as he skillfully redirects the conversation, always maintaining that positive tone.

"Bob and I always got along well. I was on his treasury team for many years, and I learned a lot from him. He's brilliant, and you're right—he's very funny." I leave it at that, also wanting to keep it positive. I understand the offer.

Greg smiles and then moves on to the next big issue: relocation. This is another potential sticking point. It is rare that any senior New York–based leader relocates to our Minneapolis subsidiary.

"You know, Art, the position is in Minneapolis. It's important that you be there. The Minneapolis staff will all be reporting to you. Then, assuming all goes well, after a year you'll be promoted to CFO, a job you'll hold for two to four years. Then you'll move back to New York for another senior role here. Of course, if you want to stay in Minneapolis, that will be an option too."

He smiles. "I'd love to have you take the job, Art. It's a great opportunity for you, and it would be good for us too. Why don't you think about it and call me if you have any questions. Sound good?"

It's both squishy and intriguing. I am not too concerned about Greg's "if all goes according to plan" condition for my getting promoted in a year. Without fully understanding what's expected, I feel confident it will work out. The company has always been fair to me. It will be a risk, perhaps even more than I realize, but I am also ready for a change. The timing is right for me to get out of my comfort zone and take a chance.

Still, I have to think through two issues more deeply: one is professional, reporting to Bob for the next year; and the other is personal, moving to Minneapolis.

I have firsthand knowledge of Bob's financial acumen, larger-than-life persona, and leadership style. He's always the smartest guy in the room, and by simply observing him over the years I learned how to think like a corporate treasurer and CFO. I am grateful for that. His instinct for injecting humor into even the most difficult situations is also a positive. Then there is the downside—as a manager he is extraordinarily demanding, hard to read, and difficult to please. Reporting to him will certainly create many anxious moments, and there's no way to prepare for that.

Assessing this trade-off, I decide that the career and learning opportunities are worth it. *Besides,* I think, *it will only be for a year.*

The second big issue is personal, and it's a higher hurdle. Neither Kate nor I want to relocate. We love our New Jersey home and community. We now have three children—Max (nine), Elena (three), and Elizabeth (four months). We've been here a decade. It's home, and we don't want to leave.

Kate had a successful career as a business strategy consultant for fifteen years. It was only recently that she put her career on hold and became a full-time mom. She has a strong local friend network and is now establishing herself as a community leader. With a young family in tow and my need to be highly focused on work, we both know Kate will bear the burden of managing our family's needs in a new home and community.

We discuss it extensively. I am ready to take the professional challenge, and relocating is unfortunately a requirement. It will be extremely disruptive for Kate. Being the supportive, unselfish partner that she is, she is open to it. Then she introduces a factor that casts a new, softer light on the question.

"You know, Art, there is something I've been thinking about that's bothering me. Ever since 9/11, I'm not comfortable living here. I don't even like going into New York City. Driving through the tunnels makes me nervous. I still don't feel safe." She pauses, quietly reflecting before continuing. "Maybe relocating would be a good idea."

Nearly a year later, the trauma from 9/11 is still fresh. We both feel it, as New York City now has a completely different vibe. Far more stringent security protocols are visible everywhere—public transportation, office buildings, sports events, public spaces—even in New Jersey. Everyone is still on edge.

She continues, "But we'll move only if this is really a good opportunity for you. Can you trust Greg to follow through on this offer?"

"Honestly, I don't know. I think so, but I just don't know."

That August (in 2002), before committing, we take a family trip to Minneapolis to get a firsthand look. A local realtor arranges a full area tour—communities, homes for sale, and schools. Our first day is a delightfully sunny, breezy summer afternoon, and she drives us down Lake Street in suburban, upscale Wayzata. There are dozens of sailboats, small white sails billowing, bouncing along the choppy blue water of Lake Minnetonka's Wayzata Bay. Flanked on the other side of Lake Street are an amalgam of attractive boutiques and casual browsers. It is tranquil and beautiful, even magical, and we are completely enchanted. This is Minnesota?

We are also impressed by the quality of life and the relatively low cost of living. We see house after house that is bigger, more modern, and more beautiful than our New Jersey home, and at considerably less cost. My commuting time in New Jersey is well over an hour each way. Wherever we settle in the Twin Cities, that will be cut in half, if not more. It is an impressive "sell" job, and we both feel any remaining resistance eroding.

As we cycle through the pluses and minuses for the umpteenth time, the one negative we keep coming back to is the winter weather. It particularly concerns Kate, who detests being cold, and finds long winters to be depressing. We recall our first-ever trip to the Twin Cities more than twenty years earlier. We drove from New York City by way of a visit to Kate's family in Detroit. As we drove farther and farther north through Wisconsin, a frozen glaze grew on the inside of all four passenger windows. It started from the outer edges and crept inexorably toward the center. As it grew and the unfrozen part of each window shrank, the outer edges got thicker and thicker. It kept growing until the insides were completely ice covered. This whole process took about two hours and was completed just as we arrived. Even growing up in New England, I had never seen anything like that.

"Take the offer, Art. It will be good to get out of the New York area, and you have an opportunity. You've always wanted a bigger CFO role. Except for the winters, I think I'll like it there. And we're planning to move back to New Jersey in a few years anyway, right?"

Extraordinarily grateful for Kate's selfless support, I take the offer, even though it means moving to a new place—a cold new place. I am anxious, determined, and also feeling guilty for uprooting Kate and our family. *This had better work out*, I quietly think.

4

DARK DAYS

Whatever it is you are seeking won't
come in the form you are expecting.

—Haruki Murakami, *Kafka on the Shore*

Immediately after accepting the job, our lives descend into a state of barely controlled turmoil. This is inevitable as we sort out all of the arrangements for finding a place to live, deciding on our kids' new school situations, figuring out what to do with our New Jersey home, and packing for a major move. Compounding these challenges are my new professional circumstances. I have little time to transition out of my old and into my new job. I step right into a pressure cooker, commuting weekly to Minneapolis for the first month and living out of a downtown hotel, as Kate and I (but mostly Kate) sort out all of the family-transition details.

We take it all on with high energy and optimism. We have to—we know this is the only way to make it work, both as a family and for each of us individually. Mentally and emotionally I am prepared for anything, and it's a good thing . . .

It's a Monday at 7 a.m. I've been on the job for just a few weeks, and I know there is a lot at stake. I look around at several of my anxious finance-team members. They sit at the oversized, circular table that dominates my office, and we review our presentation with a laser-like focus. We are tense, nervously preparing for a big day.

The corporate jet, carrying a planeload of senior American Express executives, is already airborne from its Teterboro, New Jersey, home, and is headed to Minneapolis. It carries both the parent company's executive team and Financial Advisors' handful of New York–based leaders who choose to "commute" weekly on the jet. The latter group eschewed relocating to the Twin Cities in favor of maintaining their homes in the New York City area. Bob, our interim CFO, is among this New York City-based group.

Today we will conduct a comprehensive business review with the skeptical parent-company leaders. Since the months-ago investment losses, followed by embarrassing news headlines, there is a high level of sensitivity about our plans to get back on track. Wall Street investors are watching. The new Financial Advisors' team is determined to show that we have a good plan and are capable of executing it well. The financial presentation will lead off the session, and it will set the day's tone.

While on the plane, Bob reviews the two-dozen Power Point slides my team prepared. In just three hours, Bob will present these slides to kick off the day-long meeting. I imagine that he is very upset with me, scowling at the slides, scratching notes and corrections, and creating several new slides.

"This is crap!" he undoubtedly thinks. He pulls out his phone.

"Art!" he hisses. "You have to fix these slides! The numbers don't tie out. We can't present this." Bob has an uncanny ability to spot mistakes, even obscure ones, in a set of complex financial schedules. "Oh," he adds, "and that's not all. I'm also adding several new slides. I'm faxing them over right now."

Standing in my office and eyeing the speakerphone at my table's center, I am on high alert, willing myself to stay calm and think clearly. "Bob, I saw those problems and already fixed the numbers, so we're in good shape." I feel confident, speaking to Bob as I hold eye contact with my staff members. I had been through many Bob-driven, last-minute "fire drills" in a prior company role. "But what's this about new slides?" I ask. "I need to take a look and call you back." This part makes me nervous.

We get the handwritten slides a minute later, and as I feared, they are incomprehensible. Bob may be at the top of the class for financial acumen, but communicating his demands is not his strength. His penmanship is terrible, and his mind works a hundred times faster than he writes, resulting in abrupt, abbreviated, and truncated communications.

My team and I lay the slides out, carefully studying them. We must look like a group of Talmudic scholars, leaning over my big table and scrutinizing a handwritten version of the Old Testament. After a couple of minutes of studying, we look at each other and start to argue, as Talmudic scholars might, about what Bob wants. We cannot agree, and I feel panicked, my blood pressure rising as the minutes tick away.

I call Bob to get clarification. We talk it through, and now I understand. "Bob, these new slides are a ton of work, and we have less than three hours. We have a lot of number crunching to do before we can even create them. I honestly am not sure we can get it all done." *We can't get this done in three hours. This is crazy!*

Bob can't hide his annoyance. "This is not a negotiation, Art. I need those slides done!"

"I know that, Bob. I'm not negotiating, but I want to set realistic expectations."

No response, but I know him well enough to imagine what he's thinking. *Just shut up and get to work on my slides!*

I don't know what else to say. I am in a bind as my staff watches. I don't want to set us up to fail. But I also know Bob, and he isn't going to take *no* for an answer. "Okay, Bob," I calmly continue, "we'll give it our best shot. If it's at all humanly possible, we'll get it done."

Bob isn't going to give an inch, and he immediately responds, "Don't give me that 'humanly possible' crap, Art. I need to have those slides done!"

I urgently divide up the tasks and assign them to the team. They bolt out of my office. Thirty seconds later, my HR partner, Audrey, drops in. "Art, I just saw the most amazing thing. Jim, Brian, Stephanie, and Mary ran out of your office and were sprinting down the hallway toward the elevators."

"Audrey, I can't talk. Let's catch up later." I turn to my computer. We are all on a mission, and time is of the essence. Brains racing and fingers flying across our keyboards, it is as if we all just gulped down a fistful of amphetamines.

Twenty minutes later, Bob's calling.

"Art, where are we on the slides?" he anxiously asks.

"We're on it, Bob. We're giving it our best shot. If it's humanly possible, we will get it done."

He is tense and can barely control his frustration. "Oh my God, don't give me that 'if it's humanly possible' crap again, Art!"

Twenty minutes later, there's another call from Bob. My team is present, and I put him on the speakerphone.

"Art, where are we on this?"

"We're getting there—it's going to be tight." I do a quick rundown on all the pieces that are now falling into place. "Bob, we really need to get back to this."

He hesitates a second, and then presses on, "Well, are you going to get it done?"

Exasperated, it's my turn to vent. "Yes, Bob! If it's at all humanly possible, we'll get it done!"

Oops! Bob has a temper, and I know that an explosion is imminent. This will be highly embarrassing in front of my new team.

Instead, there's silence—several seconds of silence—and it feels like minutes. We all stand motionless, looking down to avoid eye contact, dreading the inevitable. Then Bob, speaking calmly and slowly in his inimitable, deadpan style, asks, "Art, are we talking about Minnesota humans or New York humans?"

"What?" cry my half-dozen Minnesota staff members in unison. *Welcome to Bob's World,* I think, quietly thankful for the tension-busting comment.

We get it done, the presentation goes well, and in the end, all parties are relieved and satisfied. This episode has all the elements of a classic Bob encounter: a high stakes, all-hands-on-deck, drop-every-thing emergency staged at the eleventh hour; anxious staff members pushed to their limits; high drama with an uncertain outcome until the very end; and an unexpected injection of humor from Bob, punc-tuating and defusing a tense scene. I appreciate this last point, but I can't count on good endings in the future. I know that I am in for an emotional roller coaster ride this year.

These are, literally, dark days. During my initial weeks living out of a hotel, I leave for work in the darkness of early morning, navigat-ing Minneapolis's dimly lit skyways. On the way, I always pass a local bank's clock and thermometer. My indelible mental image is that it consistently shows the time and temperature to be 6:37 a.m. and thir-ty-seven degrees. It turns out to be the coldest October in a couple of decades. *Welcome to Minnesota,* I morosely tell myself, thinking ahead to the little grenades waiting to explode when I get to my office and first check my emails and voicemails. When I leave work in the evening, it is also dark.

Inheriting a demoralized team creates additional challenges. I am way out of my comfort zone but sense that I am growing into the role. Nagging doubts persist, though. The highest hurdle, as expect-ed, is managing my relationship with Bob. I value the opportunity to learn from him, but it's no picnic working for him. Our leadership styles could not be more different, presenting a yin and yang to col-leagues and subordinates. On my good days, I think this is a positive and that we're an effective, complementary team. More often, I just feel anxious and stressed. While our relationship remains mutually respectful and supportive, it is wearing me out.

I'm also starting to think that my personal style is not a good fit with the company's, particularly at the senior leadership level. Build-ing relationships with some of my peers is more difficult than expect-ed. I am an introvert who is instinctively collaborative, and it feels like I'm an outlier on both scores. I sometimes wonder if I'm failing, and I'm not sure how to turn things around.

The problem isn't a lack of effort. I maintain a sharp focus and a strict daily regimen. I'm up at five o'clock every morning and on the treadmill by quarter after five for a brisk four-mile run. I'm out the door at six thirty and at my desk to start my workday by seven o'clock. Every workday is an extended sprint. A full year passes before I even take a lunch break. I usually make it home in time for a late family dinner, though I always carry the emotional burden of work. Fueled by anxiety, I develop chronic insomnia, a condition I've never shaken. It's a grindingly difficult year.

Kate and I worry for each other. We have our hands full for completely different reasons that stem from the same overarching condition—we're both adapting to major changes that are not going well. She's missing her social network, feeling trapped through that long, first winter and spring, and constantly shuttling our children to and from one thing or another. This is not the life she imagined for herself.

As I count down to my first anniversary, when I will be in position to take the CFO role, I am worn out but fueled by hope. I consciously infuse my internal dialogue with positive self-talk. I start noticing billboards all over Minneapolis, popular at that time, that say "Tough times don't last, tough people do."

I begin to view this situation through my inner athlete's lens as an endurance test, one where persistence is the key to success. I even think back to the last-ever baseball game I pitched. It was in high school, thirty years earlier. The game was tied, 2–2, after the standard seven innings, so it went into extra innings. After each additional inning, my coach met me as I came off the field. He'd ask, "How are you feeling, Art?" It was a leading question. He was looking for a sign. Am I ready to come out, or can I keep going? Each time I confidently replied, "Good. Feelin' really good." I was wearing down, but I would not admit it, to him or to myself. There was no way I was coming out; I finish what I start. I ended up pitching fifteen innings, an unheard-of duration for a pitcher, when the game was finally called due to darkness. The score was still tied 2–2.

I am now in a different kind of game, and the rules confuse me. Early in my career, I found that when I struggled professionally, the answer was to persist—bear down even harder, just as I did as a high school athlete. For two decades, that approach had worked. This time it is backfiring. Working harder doesn't seem to help, and somehow it creates even more misery. I'm mystified and searching for other success strategies. *I can't work harder, so how can I work smarter?*

One day Bob invites me into his office for a casual lunch conversation. This is not unusual, and I have no idea what's coming. As I start the conversation with a benign question, he stops me, strikes a serious tone, and says, "Actually, that's not why we're here. We're going to talk about you."

I am eating a bag of potato chips, and I stop mid-bite. Bob rarely has the patience or interest to talk about job performance or other softer subjects. He is task focused, and our conversations are always about the next set of to-dos. Sensing that he is about to drop a bomb, I make eye contact, lower the half-bitten chip, and slowly ask, "OK, what about me?"

"Art, you've done a masterful job with the staff here. You've earned their respect, and there's been a great turnaround since you came in. Jay (the Financial Advisors' CEO), Greg, and I appreciate everything you've done. But you're not getting the CFO job. Jay and Greg want me to stay on as the full-time CFO. It's just that this is a critical time in the business, and they have confidence in me. Jay asked me to stay, and I need to be here. I am not going to let him down."

It's a jolting message. I am shocked but not surprised. Although I did not want to acknowledge it, instinctively I knew this was coming. Jay and Bob have a long history together, and they are extremely close. Bob mentored Jay early on in his career, at a time when Bob was already at a senior level and Jay was a rising star. They have a strong bond of loyalty and trust.

I rapidly process Bob's words, searching for insights and implications. I remain outwardly calm, even as my mind races, my stomach churns, and my emotions plummet. It's clear that Bob wants to stay as CFO. Jay, I have no doubt, also wants him to stay. *That's it? Now what?*

"What about Greg? Where is he on this?" I ask.

"Greg agrees with Jay and me. Jay wants me to stay. He needs me to be here. It's a critical time for the business, and Greg agrees. He knows you've worked hard and have done a good job, but he also agrees that I need to stay here for now."

"For now? For how long? What does this mean for me?" My mind is spinning. *This is the "promotion to CFO" opportunity I uprooted my family for?*

"We're reorganizing Finance to better align with our business. You're getting one of the new positions, CFO of insurance and annuities. You'll continue to report to me."

Listening intently as he goes on, I am silently, sullenly processing the real message: I didn't make the cut, plain and simple. I am being passed over. And this new job? It doesn't feel real; it feels like I'm being shoved aside.

I am angry, but mostly I'm disappointed and feeling powerless. I know that Bob, a strong inside player, holds all the cards. There is nothing more for me to say, and there's nothing to do. At least not right away.

A couple days later, I hear from Greg. We have a predictable and utterly forgettable conversation. Not unexpectedly, Greg offers soothing words, wrapped in a complimentary tone. But the message is just as devastating.

"Art, you did a great job in helping turns things around in Minneapolis. We are in a better place now than we were a year ago. But now the business is still in such a tough spot. We really need Bob to stay as the business's key Finance partner. You can take on a new role and contribute in a different way."

There it is. Notwithstanding a seemingly nice new job title, the outcome is clear: after nearly two decades of steady forward progress, my American Express career just went sideways. At this company, and at my age (forty-seven), that likely means one thing: it's over. Sure, I will continue to have a job and a paycheck, at least for a while. As for my future here, it's bleak.

5

Reflection

I felt terrible. For starters, I didn't get the promotion I relocated for and was hired to get. And while there were many factors, there was no escaping the between-the-lines message—I didn't do a good enough job to earn it. That was profoundly disheartening. It was also embarrassing, a high-profile failure. My second-guessing demons sprang to life: *Was I given a fair shot, or did I simply not step up to the role?*

And then there were the home-front issues. Kate, of course, was disappointed for me and was very supportive. I loved her dearly for that. But I felt especially bad for her. A year earlier, I asked her to make a major sacrifice, and we uprooted a comfortable life for this. For what? It weighed heavily. *Why did we sell our house in New Jersey?* We now felt stuck in Minneapolis.

Further clouding the future was my dispiriting work reality: I had no interest in my new role, I would continue to report to Bob, and the timetable was open-ended.

Questions swirled. With a new position that signaled failure, how could I maintain a positive attitude? Was my career at American Express salvageable, or should I just cut my losses and move on? Realistically, could I start fresh somewhere else at my age? Did I even want to play this corporate game anymore, here or anywhere else?

I was in full existential career-crisis mode. How did I get here?

Did I not assess this opportunity critically enough a year earlier? Was it as simple as me having made a bad decision? Did I trust naively when I shouldn't have? Or did I simply reach my level of incompetence and fall back? What should I have done differently? What could I have done better?

I didn't have answers.

Throughout my life, I confidently navigated challenges of all kinds—career, relationships, personal health, whatever. I always trusted my decision-making instincts and felt they served me well.

Until now.

Maybe it's because I always had a smooth, undisturbed path—raised in a stable home, happily married, and never having suffered a significant personal trauma such as a divorce, layoff, or health crisis. Both my personal life and career had consistently trended positive.

Until now.

Was I lucky for my blessed life? I was certainly grateful for it.

Or was I unlucky that I had not been severely tested, even once, and had not learned how to be more resilient? More hard-headed? To think and judge more critically?

My personal identity was wrapped up in my career success—too wrapped up, and it was bringing me down. That was the core issue. What had, for two decades, felt like professional success now felt like personal failure.

Among other things, this was a test of character. The immediate priority was to outwardly meet the moment with grace—to demonstrate resilience and equanimity—regardless of what my gut was feeling. I had to show up for my new job at American Express with a positive attitude and maintain it as I tried to figure out next steps. It would be difficult, but it was the only viable choice.

Then there was the more complicated and critical issue—what to do about my future, with my American Express career likely on a dead-end path. Jumping to another company was the easy answer. Would that fix the problem? I was skeptical and vaguely felt that I was looking for something else—there had to be something else—but I didn't know what. A different employer, like a Band-Aid, would have provided short-term relief, but it would not have cured what I sensed was a greater underlying ailment. The search for answers would take time and would require patience.

In *The Tempest,* one of William Shakespeare's characters stated, "What is past is prologue," creating context to help explain the future. This resonated with me. I was emotionally unsettled as I began puzzling over my own future, vaguely recognizing the need to reboot—to redefine a set of professional and personal objectives that suddenly, and traumatically, were unclear. My past—growing up in a completely different world of simple home comforts and strong community ties—would provide insights and navigational guidance.

PART II

Foundations

6

MOM AND DAD

I can't give you anything but love, baby.
That's the only thing I've plenty of, baby . . .
—Jimmy McHugh and Dorothy Fields,
"I Can't Give You Anything but Love"

Kate, whom I met long after leaving my New London, Connecticut, childhood home, once jokingly shared that her vision of my early home life was a setting from the 1960s television sitcom *Leave It to Beaver.* It was complete with a stable, supportive family, a stay-at-home mom, wise-cracking friends, kids who made money by delivering the daily newspaper on their bicycles, and a setting where there were no problems that couldn't be resolved within the confines of a thirty-minute television show.

There's some truth to her perception. Mom and Dad were traditional parents in the best sense of the word, creating a household island of emotional stability, encouragement, and unconditional love. As exemplary role models, they taught my siblings and me to support each other, to strive for academic success, to think critically, and to actively engage in our community. They also encouraged us to nurture interests outside the classroom as the way to experience life more fully. Developing "well-rounded" children was a core parenting principle.

Lessons learned from Mom and Dad were formative. In recent years, I've come to better understand how they influenced every important decision I've made, right through my professional career and well beyond.

My mom, Bernice, grew up in Great Depression–era Brooklyn and had a privileged childhood. Her father, my grandpa Joe, was a first-generation eastern European Jewish immigrant with an iron will, a gift for gab, and entrepreneurial talent. He was a successful flour broker with an office in lower Manhattan and a seat on the New York Mercantile Exchange. They lived in a magnificent six-bedroom home in Brooklyn's Midwood neighborhood, where her family also had a live-in maid.

The Great Depression eventually took its toll, though, and Grandpa Joe lost his fortune in 1939 when Mom was sixteen years old. The day she graduated high school, they moved from their six-bedroom house into a small, four-room, second-floor walk-up apartment in Far Rockaway, Queens. Mom then slept on a cot in a bedroom she shared with her sister. My grandpa's friends counseled him to declare bankruptcy in order to relieve his obligation to pay off a staggering amount of debt. He steadfastly refused. According to Mom, he thought declaring bankruptcy was dishonorable and that it would forever taint his reputation. He ended up paying back all of his debts, though it took many years.

Mom was a brilliant and ambitious student, graduating high school two years ahead of her peers. But she did not apply to college. College was not a common choice for girls in the late 1930s, and her family could not afford college tuition. Her parents expected her to work in a New York City department store just like her older sister, my aunt Ethel. Mom desperately wanted to go to college, and she enlisted her Yale-educated older brother, my uncle Henry, to convince my grandparents that she needed to go. It worked. Mom applied to the University of Connecticut during the summer of 1939 and matriculated that fall. Even though he had no money and was already deeply in debt, my grandpa borrowed the entire $300 needed to cover Mom's college tuition.

Mom was eight years younger than Dad, but they both graduated from the University of Connecticut in 1943. Oddly enough, they didn't know each other then and wouldn't meet for another four years. From college, Mom went directly for a master's degree in sociology at the University of Wisconsin. It was the mid-1940s, and following graduation, Mom was told that aspiring career women had two viable paths: they could be nurses or teachers. Mom chose to teach.

It was difficult for women to find university teaching jobs in the 1940s. She always competed against men, and more than once she was told that even though she was the best candidate, a man would get the job. After all, as she was once told, "men have families to support. If you got the job, you'd just go off and get married, have children, and drop out of work."

She was disappointed but also somewhat ambivalent. She understood the reasoning. "After all," she rationalized, "the men *did* have families to support, and I did plan to get married, have children, and be a full-time mom." I always found this to be interesting, as in my lifetime, she had strong, progressive views on the need for women to have equal access to professional opportunities.

Her first teaching job out of graduate school was in Tallahassee, Florida, at Florida State College for Women (which in the late 1940s became part of Florida State University). She stayed for one year and disliked it. She was repulsed by realities of the Jim Crow South, such as "whites only" and "colored only" public bathrooms and drinking fountains. Her next job was at the University of Connecticut's Fort Trumbull branch in New London. It was there that she met Dad.

This was 1947, and UConn's Fort Trumbull branch was a university outpost established for a short period of time to accommodate the demand from returning World War II veterans. Veterans were taking advantage of the G.I. Bill to fund their educations and were going to college in droves. Mom and Dad met in September of their first year teaching at Fort Trumbull. Two weeks after that first meeting, they were engaged, and three months later, they married. They stayed married until Dad's death in 2006.

Dad loved to tell stories of how Mom dazzled him from the

start—it was her shy but engaging personality, sense of humor, intellect, and good looks. He knew instantly that she was the one. He and his single teaching colleagues, all of whom were men except for Mom, used to hang out together and go to restaurants and bars. There was one car in the group, and there were more bodies than seats. Dad always managed to get her to sit on his lap for the ride. He showed undisguised delight in describing those rides. Mom confessed that she, too, enjoyed them.

True to their goals and values, my parents started a family shortly after getting married. Mom chose to stay home for more than fifteen years in order to raise their three children. During that time, she also worked part-time as a substitute teacher, a Hebrew School teacher, and a private tutor for high school students. She eventually went back to full-time teaching. I vividly remember those early tutoring sessions, mostly because the kitchen, which doubled as her office, became strictly off-limits. That was quite a constraining factor on weekday evenings for a chronic food scavenger like myself, but it was just part of growing up, and I never gave it a second thought.

Although her master's degree was in sociology, she pivoted later in life and became a high school math teacher. Mom excelled in just about every subject. She was the family's intellectual—highly literate, engaged in the world, current on public issues, and willing to enthusiastically converse on any topic. News radio (WCBS from New York) was always on in our kitchen, and she loved to have us join her in watching talk and news shows on public television. The Sunday New York Times was required reading in our house. Mom hungrily consumed the Sunday Magazine, and then she'd ace the impossibly difficult crossword puzzle.

Mom's reputation among her teacher colleagues was the female equivalent of a *mensch*—kind, humble, empathetic, and a great friend and mentor. Many of the teachers were drawn to Mom as their go-to colleague for advice. Following Mom's retirement in 1986, one younger teacher who had adopted Mom as a surrogate parent sent her a Mother's Day card every year for thirty-three years, right up until one week before Mom's death in 2019 at the age of ninety-six.

When Mom was in her late eighties, she chaired the Democratic Party in a large retirement community. In that capacity, she once moderated a gubernatorial debate for the state of Virginia. One of the debaters, who would eventually become governor, attempted to intimidate her. The debate's start was delayed due to a tardy participant, and he got right in her face, threatening that he would leave if they didn't start immediately. She didn't give an inch and replied, "You can leave if you'd like, and if you do, I'm going to tell everyone in the audience that you chose to walk out on them. And you know what? Every one of us old people votes." Then she walked away. He, of course, stayed.

Dad admiringly called her a "tough cookie." She was also a loving parent—a patient, respectful, and humble woman who unfailingly subordinated her own needs over her lifetime for her family's, especially for her children (and, later in life, for her grandchildren).

Dad grew up in more modest circumstances than Mom. His family had a small house in the ethnically and racially diverse community of Bridgeport, Connecticut. His father, Harry, also a first-generation Jewish immigrant from eastern Europe, was a tailor and made a pittance. Harry had a big heart and in the depths of the Great Depression was reluctant to take payment for his work. It was his way to help others. Following my dad's high school graduation in 1932, he became the family's primary income earner. Dad delayed starting college for eight years in order to support his family.

He was always a devoted son, even later in his life. One of my earliest childhood memories is of Dad taking care of his ailing elderly mother, my grandma. She lived in what we then called a "convalescent home" in New Haven, fifty miles from our New London home. Every weekend, he made the trip to see her for an afternoon. He would bribe me into going with him by promising to take me out for an ice cream sundae. Al's Restaurant on Whalley Avenue is burned into my memory, with its speckled, brick-red Formica tabletops, booths, and picture-perfect ice cream sundaes. They were served in classic, old-fashioned parfait glasses with whipped cream and a cherry on top. I learned over time that Dad enjoyed these outings as much as I did.

As a second-generation American, he described his Bridgeport community with great affection as a classic "melting pot" of lower- and middle-class immigrants, a place comprised of eastern European Jews, people from Ireland, Italy, and Poland, and African Americans who were migrating from the South. He had a knack for getting along with everyone. He proudly talked about his Bridgeport schools, and he attended his Bridgeport Central High School reunions until he was well into his eighties.

We often teased Dad that he didn't graduate college until he was nearly thirty years old because he wasn't too smart. He countered, with a twinkle in his eye, that being an older college student "gave me an advantage with the ladies." He asserted that he was a "big man on campus." We, of course, didn't believe him, and it became a family joke. Then one day we came across his college yearbook and were shocked to see the words "Big Man on Campus" under his picture.

Whereas Mom was more outwardly warm, intellectual, and serious, Dad was the parent who could inject levity into any situation. He was the family character, possessing a natural sense of humor. He had a gift for seeing the lighter side in any situation, whether it was in an explicit joke or just in his bearing. He had a gentle spirit and carried that lightness with him in a delightful way. He elevated the mood of a room just by being there. Although he was generally quiet, he could also be very social.

He had an oddly charming quality of being funny without trying. He fractured the English language, sometimes without realizing it, and other times quite deliberately. He was famously terrible with names, consistently coming close but getting them wrong. He even got his kids' names wrong. Occasionally when calling out to me, he'd say "Oh Henry, Laura, Bernice, I-mean-Art," ticking off every family name in rapid succession until he reached mine. He also had a way for twisting words and ideas, like when he referred to one of my early career roles as being a "management insultant," or when he greeted

Mom on the morning of her sixty-fifth birthday by saying "Welcome to Club Med." Upon returning home from golfing during his later years, he would characterize his day by saying one of two things: "I was the Bob Berman of old," which meant he played well, or "I was the old Bob Berman," meaning he played poorly. He never directly admitted his age, but he did offer a clue when he shared on each successive birthday which anniversary of his thirty-ninth birthday he was celebrating.

He had the opposite of an adventurous spirit. If we went out to dinner, he always ordered the same thing. At Chinese restaurants, it was *moo goo gai pan,* which he referred to as "goo goo gai pan." And for dessert, he had vanilla ice cream. When we visited Howard Johnson's, which famously advertised its twenty-eight flavors of ice cream, he would intensely study the list of flavors before making his decision. "C'mon, Dad, we know you're getting vanilla." And he always did. Dad was not a risk-taker, and we teased him for it all the time. He was a good sport.

Music was a big deal in our family, and it was one of Dad's unabashed loves. One of his all-time favorite gifts was an orchestra conductor's baton. He loved to stand in the living room, put his favorite symphony records on, and conduct the orchestra. We had a large caricature drawing of the famous conductor Arturo Toscanini hanging over our piano. In Dad's mind, he was transported to being the great Toscanini, complete with wildly flowing white hair. His body moved in smooth rhythm and rapturous joy, eyes closed and a soft smile on his face.

Aside from family and music, golfing was his passion. It seems odd that a poor, Depression-era boy growing up in a lower-middle-class urban community got into golf. But one of the many jobs he had as a boy was to caddy at a local country club. As a caddy, he would sneak onto the golf course with borrowed clubs to play early and late, and he fell in love with the game—and boy did he have game. He played golf with an unforgettable quiet intensity. It was unlike him, I thought. But this was another side of him that rarely showed—his competitiveness. He had confidence, and he loved to compete, especially against guys he considered to be overly cocky or smart alecks. He was a modest guy, and he disliked those who lacked humility, guys who "tooted their own horns." I think he figured he was doing the world a favor by "taking them down a peg or two" (as Mom would say), and he took quiet satisfaction in beating them.

Family and golf, in that order, were his top priorities. Before he and Mom got married, he told her he needed to disclose something very important about himself, and that they needed to sit down and talk. Since they did not yet know each other well, Mom was worried. *Uh oh, this was too good to be true, and now I'm going to hear about the real Bob Berman.*

He shared that he needed her blessing to spend several hours every Saturday and Sunday playing golf. "Bernice, I'm not a womanizer, gambler, or drinker, and I'll be a dedicated husband and father. But I have to play golf every week, twice a week. That's really important to me, and you need to know that." He was nervous about asserting this need, but he was insistent. Mom was relieved. *This is his big disclosure?* And true to his word, Dad played golf at least twice a week throughout his life. Mom was okay with that.

Work was a means to an end for Dad. This attitude, I believe, was shaped by his family's Depression-era struggles. Having a job was an economic necessity; a steady paycheck was reason enough to be thankful. On-the-job satisfaction was nice to have but was not expected or even necessary. That view endured through his adult life.

Following a brief period teaching math and engineering, he was a sonar engineer for the U.S. Navy and became a career civil servant. He was our family's financial provider. Work, for Dad, was all about the financial security derived from a steady paycheck. He rarely discussed his job; it enabled us to afford a comfortable middle-class lifestyle, and that's what mattered. While Dad did not seem to enjoy work, particularly in the later years of his work life, he never complained. He put in steady eight-hour days, and not a minute longer. Non-work time was for family and golf.

Mom and Dad seemed to have a good marriage. Dad would occasionally tell my brother and me, with a sparkle in his eyes, that "you'd be lucky if you ever marry a woman half as nice as Mom." His favorite song was "I Can't Give You Anything but Love," famously performed by Louis Armstrong, and he would often sing it to Mom. Characteristically, he never got the words quite right. Always close, and always capturing the spirit, but not quite right.

My parents made a point not to fight or even argue in front of the children. I cannot recall a single angry exchange between them. It did not occur to me until I was much older that this suppression of conflict, though it made for a low-drama household, also created a sense of unreality.

Personal values were not something we talked about; they never said, "this is the way you should behave." Mom and Dad just lived their values, modeling honesty, compassion, and empathy. There were no gray areas. One example is when I qualified for financial aid to go to college. Dad would not accept the grant. He asserted, "There are other people who need the money more than we do, so we shouldn't take it." He ended up paying every penny of my college education. It was a source of pride for him.

This ethic carried over to their material values, which were straight-up utilitarian. One of Mom's mantras was "If you don't need it, why buy it?" Clothes were kept until we grew out of them or until they were just worn out; blue jeans, which we called dungarees, were patched rather than replaced; cars were run until they broke down and were no longer serviceable; and we dutifully collected and redeemed S&H Green Stamps in order to get free retail items.

Simple household appliances were used until they stopped working. Even then, we often continued to use them. The "on" lever on our toaster would not stay depressed unless we manually held it down. For years, Dad would regularly stand at the kitchen counter, finger remaining on the lever, and have casual conversations with us until the toast was done.

I took all of this for granted as a boy. It wasn't until early adulthood that I realized growing up sheltered in this warm emotional bubble, with its strong moral core, was a great and rare gift.

I learned it had a downside too. As a younger adult, I felt lost when directly addressing certain stressful situations. Dealing effectively with conflict and being comfortable with healthy confrontation were hard for me. I was ill-equipped in dealing with people driven by ego, narcissism, selfishness, or greed.

7

HOME COMFORTS IN A HARDSCRABBLE CITY

Give me the child until he is seven,
and I will show you the man.

—Aristotle

Kate's comparison of my early home life as a cutout from the antiseptic, soft fuzziness of *Leave It to Beaver* was half joking, half serious, a nod to my parents' sincere and successful attempt to create a warm home environment. It only goes so far, though, and thank goodness for that.

Stepping outside the immediate Berman household is where the comparison to the Beaver's idealized world abruptly ended. The broader social context for my childhood was Civil Rights–era New London, Connecticut, in the 1960s, not the Beaver's antiseptic Mayfield. New London was a rich, simmering stew of socioeconomic and racial diversity, social change, and community unrest. It had idiosyncratic character and the types of tough challenges faced by many urban areas.

The *New York Times* real estate section described New London as a "hardscrabble, blue collar city." I had to look up the word *hardscrabble*, but I immediately got the point. The Times' article's judgment felt a little harsh, though it was a common perspective. New London was distinctly working- and middle-class and could appear rough around the edges to outsiders. It also has a rich pre–Revolutionary War history, a diverse population, and an unpretentious attitude. Its historic downtown and shoreline beauty add to its distinctive character. New Londoners are proud people, and we have a strong sense of place. I haven't lived in New London for over four decades, but I still feel deeply rooted there.

New London was a major beneficiary of the Cold War. Starting in the late 1940s, it developed a powerful military-industrial complex, particularly for such a relatively small area. The area's biggest employer, a division of General Dynamics, was the country's largest nuclear submarine builder. At its height, it employed over thirty-thousand people, equal to New London's total population. Employees were mostly union-dues-paying tradesmen. General Dynamics offered on-the-job training to high school students, and many of my high school classmates skipped college in favor of apprenticeship employment. It offered union membership, job security, and a path to a comfortable middle-class life.

The area is also home to the U.S. Coast Guard Academy and the U.S. Navy's largest submarine base. Dad's job as a sonar engineer for nearly thirty years was with a U.S. Navy research facility, where he helped develop sonar technology to track enemy submarines. His office was located on the site of the temporary University of Connecticut branch where he and Mom met—on the Thames River, adjacent to Fort Trumbull, a Revolutionary War–era fort. The research lab has long since closed down, but Fort Trumbull remains a tourist attraction.

At just six square miles, New London was one of the most densely populated of all of Connecticut's 169 cities and towns. It had problems common to many urban areas. What had been southeastern Connecticut's commercial hub was fast becoming a shell by the time I reached high school in the early 1970s. The once-thriving downtown had mostly vacant storefronts, thanks to the area's first shopping mall opening on I-95, just two miles away. Also, because New London had a high density of tax-exempt institutions—churches and synagogues, public schools, parochial schools, colleges and significant military presence; a weak commercial sector within the city limits; a tiny geographic footprint; and a generally middle- and lower-middle-class population, it had a small tax base. Public services were chronically starved for funding. Mom was a leader in the local teachers' union, and the perennial public school funding battles were a regular source of household conversation.

New London's public school system had one public high school and one public junior high school. They were fed by six neighborhood elementary schools. While attending elementary school, I learned a new term that was part of New London's public lexicon: *de facto* segregation. I lived in a predominantly white neighborhood and attended the elementary school in the area with the least racial diversity and the highest density of professional people.

Although my neighborhood was almost entirely white, New London, overall, was diverse—economically, racially, ethnically, and religiously. If you were African American or Puerto Rican (the area's predominant immigrant community at that time) and you lived anywhere in eastern Connecticut, New London was likely your home. Similar to Dad's Bridgeport home but on a smaller scale, there were also a lot of white ethnic groups in New London—Italian, Polish, Greek, and many others. There was a sizable Jewish population as well. Areas with low-income housing projects, duplex homes, and small single-family houses flowed continuously throughout many parts of the city.

New London is also blessed with a couple miles of shoreline where the Thames River, Long Island Sound, and Atlantic Ocean converge. The areas that are immediately adjacent to the water have magnificent homes. Abraham Ribicoff, a former senator, governor, and member of President Kennedy's cabinet, owned one of them.

A ten-minute walk from the waterfront, our steepled, three-bedroom Dutch Colonial–style house was comfortably nestled in a middle-class neighborhood. Living in a 1,400-square-foot house, our family of five had little room to spare. The only place for a television was in the corner of our dining room, and a baby grand piano took up half of the living room. It didn't strike us as abnormal that everyone in the house could hear Dad snoring at night, or that only my sister,

Laura, had her own bedroom. The one day-to-day reality that we still marvel about decades later is how we all managed to share one small bathroom and still live in peace. I was the acknowledged bathroom hog, and since I was the youngest, this became a family joke (except, of course, during the times when I was actually hogging the bathroom, which particularly annoyed Mom).

Encouraging the kids' interest in extracurriculars, especially music and sports, was a parenting priority. All three of us took piano lessons from a proper British lady, the infamous Mrs. Hart. She was strict and very intimidating. I had to prepare for a humiliating scolding if my practice log did not show at least one hour of practice every day, including lesson day. I reengaged in playing as a late-middle-aged adult, and when I described Mrs. Hart's personality and teaching style to my current piano teacher, her response was, "She must be German." Two years later, not remembering this conversation, I made another reference to Mrs. Hart's teaching style, and she said, "She must be Russian." Even Mom, no shrinking violet, was intimidated by Mrs. Hart. When Mom reluctantly called to cancel a lesson for a legitimate reason, like illness, Mrs. Hart was quite displeased, and she let Mom know it.

Mrs. Hart was highly structured and utterly humorless. Her annual highlight was a student recital at the massive Second Congregational Church on Broad Street, where she played as church organist on Sundays. Preparing for those recitals was excruciating. During the final week, we did the dreaded countdown, where we would start at one hundred and play our piece a hundred times before recital time. We had to write down the countdown number after each rendition until we reached zero. In those days, everything had to be memorized. At the recital itself, the programs indicated how many pieces each student had memorized and could play at recital-level quality. The best students had ten, fifteen, or even twenty. I was always a little embarrassed to have only two or three next to my name. I lasted just three years with Mrs. Hart.

Mom felt that the different ways each of us reacted to the rigors of Mrs. Hart's piano lessons provided a sharp lens into our personalities: my sister, Laura, would sometimes come out of lessons crying because she was sensitive; my brother, Henry, would come out of lessons angry because he was emotional; and I would come out of lessons with a relieved smile because I wouldn't have to do this for another whole week. Mom saw that as pragmatism.

Piano concertos, Broadway standards, upbeat jazzy tunes, or anything from the Great American Songbook were a constant in our home, either being played on our piano or listened to on our hi-fi living room record player. Everyone especially loved the musical stage show recordings. We knew them all and never got tired of listening—*West Side Story*, everyone's favorite; *The King and I, South Pacific, Fiddler on the Roof, Man of La Mancha, Mame, Cabaret, The Sound of Music* . . . the list goes on and on. Mom and Dad gave Laura a Lerner and Loewe piano book inscribed with the words, "To Our Fair Lady on her 13th Birthday." We still have that book. We also have an old Rodgers and Hammerstein compendium that I pull out on occasion.

While I enjoyed music, it was playing sports, particularly team sports, that was always my number one passion. It gave me unadulterated joy, and a love for participation sports has lasted a lifetime. Working hard with teammates toward a common goal, forming enduring friendships, and opening doors to new people and experiences—what could be better? Five decades removed from my youth, I still self-identify as an athlete. I also know that at my current age (mid-sixties), calling myself an athlete requires considerable magical thinking.

I shared my childhood sports obsession, particularly baseball and basketball, with my next-door neighbor and best buddy, Eric Olsen. The season of the year, rain or shine, darkness or light, the actual sport itself—none of that mattered—we were outside playing. Our outdoor space was "sports central" for our friends over the years. There could not have been a better place for sports-minded boys to grow up.

The Olsens had two boys; Eric was my age, and Martin was a couple of years older. The Olsens and the Bermans were like second families to each other. Eric and I were close, and Martin and Henry were close. Our moms were best friends, and our dads were golfing buddies. Eric and Martin felt to me like brothers, and Mr. and Mrs. Olsen were second parents to the Berman kids.

Our families were polar opposites in many ways. The Olsens were "old school." They had strict parenting styles and were politically conservative, while the Bermans were more lenient, progressive, and liberal. We understood those differences, and none of it mattered. The bond we shared was based on mutual respect, affection, and shared interests. Our families both had strong family- and community-focused values. We shared accomplishments and joys over the years, as well as disappointments and tragedies. We all regularly dropped in unannounced at each other's houses, kids and parents alike, and we always looked out for each other.

Core to our personal and community values was Mom and Dad's connection to Judaism. We were members of New London's conservative Jewish congregation, and all of the children went to Hebrew School from an early age. As kids, religion was a part of our lives, although not a central part. We attended synagogue on the high holidays and occasionally on Sabbath and other holidays. We had wonderful family traditions for celebrating Passover with extended family and Hanukkah at home. Although we were not very religiously observant, we strongly identified as being Jewish and were proud to be part of the local Jewish community.

While maintaining their Jewish identities, Mom and Dad also thought that contributing to New London's diverse secular community was important too. This was one of their strong core beliefs, and we discussed it often.

The Berman family celebrated Christmas every year with the Olsens. I visited their house on Christmas mornings, excited to see what gifts Santa Claus left for me under their tree. I also could not wait to play with their boys' new toys. The rest of my family would come over later, everyone would exchange gifts, and the grown-ups would drink eggnog and rum.

Many of my earliest friends were Jewish, although that changed over time as my world expanded beyond the neighborhood. A close friend and I had a joint Bar Mitzvah party at our synagogue. We invited a large swath of seventh graders, which was a diverse group, both religiously and racially. We had a live band, dancing, and lots of food, and everyone had a great time.

A week or two after our party, our new rabbi asked the two of us to meet him in his office. We did not know why we were meeting and felt intimidated as the meeting began. His office overflowed with musty books, and it was a little too dark, small, and intimate. The air was a little too stale. It felt creepy.

The rabbi told us, gently but firmly, how it was a bad idea to have non-Jewish friends at our party. "Dancing with non-Jewish girls is like going out on a date, and dating non-Jewish girls leads to relationships, marriage, and non-Jewish children." This was a powerful message that Jewish people understood, even thirteen-year-olds. The logic was, if we engage in this behavior, the number of Jews will shrink, and Judaism's survival will be at risk. This was a sobering message at a time when memories of the Holocaust were still fresh for my parents' generation. Mom and Dad always made sure we were well aware of this history. I felt awful.

I was relieved that my parents were upset with the rabbi. "Why did he lay this guilt on a thirteen-year-old boy? Why didn't he come and talk to us first?" Mom said angrily. The rabbi's message also conflicted with their personal values of engaging in our secular community, even while continuing to be active members of the Jewish community.

Two years later, in the early 1970s, my sister, Laura, and her future husband, George, got engaged. George is not Jewish, and I had no idea what an issue interfaith marriage could be until they were planning their wedding. No rabbi within seventy-five miles would agree to officiate their wedding ceremony.

More difficult, even, than the planning challenges were the community attitudes that Mom and Dad faced. At High Holiday services that year, the rabbi gave a stern lecture on the dangers of interfaith relationships. "This risks the survival of Judaism," he said. "All good Jews should be alarmed by the increase in interfaith marriage, and we cannot condone it." Although there were more than five hundred people in attendance, Mom and Dad felt the rabbi was speaking to them, attempting to shame them for being bad parents and bad Jews.

They were humiliated and had little choice but to sit there and take it. After the sermon, Mom was shaking with anger. She took it personally, feeling attacked and betrayed in our community where she loyally served. In my lifetime, I never saw her so upset. I know it's something she never forgot.

I don't know how Mom and Dad initially processed Laura's interfaith engagement. If they were concerned, it never showed. They always seemed very happy for Laura and very welcoming to George.

A decade later, we relived this drama in a very small way when Kate, who is Catholic, and I got engaged and married. By that time, attitudes were changing. It helped that Kate and I both lived in a liberal pocket of Washington, DC. We planned our own wedding there and had the good fortune to find a Reformed rabbi and a Jesuit priest who tag-teamed interfaith weddings all the time. Mom and Dad could not have been more supportive or more welcoming to Kate.

In 1968, at the age of twelve, I left my comfortable, mostly white neighborhood elementary school for the city's racially integrated junior high. The social context of the time mattered a lot, even to seventh graders like me. The Vietnam War was raging, urban areas across the country were simmering with unrest, Martin Luther King Jr. was assassinated that spring, and Richard Nixon was first elected president in the fall. At the summer Olympic Games, American athletes Tommie Smith and John Carlos medaled in the 200 meters. On the podium, during the National Anthem, they bowed their heads and raised gloved fists. Although still only a preteen, I was acutely attuned to current events.

Though racially mixed, New London was not well integrated. At New London High School, there were several interracial dating couples—something that was becoming less rare but was still socially taboo. Racial controversy was further stirred by one of the school's deans, who felt it was her job to contact the white parents of students in interracial relationships. This provoked outrage in the Black community and among high school students. When Martin Luther King Jr. was assassinated in the spring, the school's principal condemned the violence on the public address system and asked that everyone work together through the tragedy. Black students and teachers were openly weeping, and many Black students believed that the school did not sufficiently honor Dr. King. They organized a walkout during school hours, and about fifty students marched downtown. There was no violence, but the community, especially the white business community, was unnerved in light of the violence taking place in other cities.

As a seventh grader new to an integrated school, I was acutely aware of racial sensitivities and fears. We all came from more homogenous neighborhood elementary schools, and most initially felt uncomfortable in this integrated setting. I certainly did. There was occasional racial tension among the kids, though public conflict was rare. My most memorable experience was later in high school, when our football team had an away game in Hartford. The Hartford fans stoned the football players' and marching band's buses. Fortunately, no one was hurt. That year, as a member of the basketball team, we played our home game against Hartford in an empty gym, for fear that allowing fans in would be inviting trouble.

Racial identity awareness was a hot topic in high school. It was often openly discussed, both casually and more formally, including in mixed racial group settings. On my ninth-grade basketball team, we had season-long locker room banter—always jokingly, it seemed—about which was better, being Black or being white. The team was about half and half by race. The conversations were grossly politically incorrect by today's standards, and thinking about that today feels strange. At the time, though, it didn't feel that way. It felt like nothing more than a bunch of teenage guys teasing and one-upping each other, and in a way that was safe in a locker room setting. I don't recall anybody having discomfort, and we played as a highly competitive, cohesive team.

This is not to say that it was always copacetic. A couple years later, before practice began on a high school team that by then was predominantly Black, I occasionally observed during practice warm-ups that the white players were shooting at one basket by ourselves, and the Black players were all shooting at the other baskets. That was a little strange, and once I noticed it, I would self-consciously switch to another basket.

My closest friend on the high school team was Vic. We had a lot in common as players—similar in size and skill—and we often went head-to-head in practice. We developed a strong mutual respect. Another reason we became friends was that we shared a frustration of not getting enough playing time. We griped on the bench together. Vic chronically complained that his playing time was curtailed because the coach was reluctant to play five Black players at the same time. According to Vic's theory, the coach always played at least one white guy (there were three of us on a team of twelve), even if it was not warranted from a game strategy perspective. I disagreed with Vic, as our coach's substitution decisions seemed logical to me. It was a memorable early lesson in how two reasonable people with dissimilar experiences and backgrounds (in this case, different races) could observe the same facts and draw opposing conclusions. Still, I was troubled by Vic's point of view and its possible implications. I sometimes wondered, *Could he be right?*

Our team was one of the top-rated in Connecticut. We had a year-end celebratory banquet sponsored by the Knights of Columbus, and it was attended by a bunch of mostly white men in the community. When our coach was acknowledged, he received a standing ovation from everyone except the players themselves. We all politely applauded, but we also all stayed planted in our seats. It was an uncomfortable moment, and everyone took note that the players showed less enthusiasm for our coach. Dad told me afterward that the guy he sat with, a local political leader, had a notably repugnant response: "What do you expect from a bunch of *schvartzes*?"

Vic and I also share a memory that is well preserved in family lore. One summer evening, my brother, Henry, and I had a chance meeting with Vic and his cousin, Mark, at Ocean Beach Park. This was our city beach. Everybody hung out at the beach in the summertime, and Henry worked evenings there. The four of us, all competitive athletes with friendly and mutually respectful relationships, got to talking. Somehow it took on an edgier, trash-talking tone. Mark was an instinctive trash talker.

"C'mon, Hank, you and your brother can't hang with Vic and me. If we played you, we'd kick your asses," he good-naturedly asserted.

My brother smiled and said, "That's bullshit, Mark, and you know it."

Vic and I looked at each other, not sure where this was going.

"Of course we would," Mark shot back. "Of course we would," he repeated. "Let's find out. Okay? Let's find out. Let's meet tonight and play. Let's play and find out. How about in a half hour at the Ocean Avenue courts?"

"I'm still working, Mark. It's only nine o'clock. I can't play now."

"When are you off work?"

"Eleven thirty."

"Good. Midnight. We'll play at midnight."

Henry looked at me inquisitively. He was clearly game. "Art, are you in?"

"Definitely," I said without hesitation. I never turned down a chance to play ball.

That was it. The two-on-two basketball showdown was set for midnight. This was a quintessential New London, 1970s scenario: a casual but highly competitive game where friends off the court were fierce competitors on it. Family and personal pride were at stake. Mark and Vic were both high-achieving, three-sport athletes in high school, and they were very cocky (as Dad would say).

After Mark and Vic left, Henry turned to me, already strategizing, and asked, "Art, how are we going to do this?"

"Vic and I will neutralize each other," I replied. "It's gonna come down to you and Mark. What do you think?"

"I think we'll take 'em. Mark has no outside shot, and he doesn't play good D."

We were excited to take them on, especially because of Mark's motor mouth. Vic was a friend, but the competitive juices flowed on both sides, and even he talked trash when he left. We knew that it was a winnable game. Mom thought we were nuts, but Dad's eyes twinkled with delight as we headed out into the darkness shortly before midnight. He wanted to come watch.

Because we all had a passion for playing basketball, it never occurred to us that a lack of court lights could be a barrier. There were several dim lights from a nearby parking lot and the adjacent street, but there were no lights on the court. Eventually our eyes adjusted as best they could. We had all played in darkness before, though I never *started* a game in the dark. It lent a surreal aura to the event.

We had an intense series of games. Mark and Vic played an aggressive, driving style. My primary visual memories, aside from the eerie sight of dim, fleeting shadows in nonstop motion, was of Vic skying for rebounds, and of Mark constantly driving hard to the basket with Henry draped all over him. Mark's lack of an outside game was their undoing. They put us to the test, but we ultimately prevailed.

Over a decade later, Vic and I reconnected at an Air Force base where he was stationed. We played some ball and reminisced, recounting New London basketball memories. Our bond from high school playing days and our love for competitive sports was still strong. I treasure the relationships that I formed through team sports. For that and many other reasons, teamwork has been a lifelong value.

Growing up in New London's social and cultural mosaic enriched me. It taught me healthy lessons about the world and my place in it. I strongly identified with my community and felt like I belonged. It continues to define and positively influence me.

Yet by the time I was in high school, I also could not wait to leave. The idea of settling there after completing my education never occurred to me. It felt too small and confining. When I left town for college in the fall of 1974, my New London days were over. I was ready to explore a larger world.

8

KATE

Night and day, you are the one
Only you beneath the moon
Under the sun . . .
—Cole Porter, "Night and Day"

August 1980.

It was only seven-thirty in the morning, and strolling the three blocks to my bus stop, I already felt the oppressive heat and humidity of a Washington, DC, summer morning. The sun cast a hazy, sultry glow on my quiet Glover Park neighborhood of tree-lined streets and tightly clustered brick townhomes. The sound of cicadas filled the air.

I had just started a new life chapter in this beautiful city, and I was brimming with optimism. I completed my MBA three months earlier, culminating six straight years of higher education. It was my second week working for the U.S. Environmental Protection Agency's economic analysis staff, and at the age of twenty-three, I had my first full-time professional job.

The bus stop was where both Benton Street and Tunlaw Road gently slope down and intersect. As I expectantly peered up Tunlaw looking for the bus, I saw a woman strolling down the street. She was striking, young, and smartly dressed in a cream-colored silk blouse, sharply creased, dark maroon slacks, and heels. She had shoulder-length chestnut brown hair with a stylish blown-dry look. She smiled easily as she crossed Benton and confidently strode right up to me, hazel eyes sparkling.

"Good morning, do you have change for the bus?"

"I think so." I stuck my hand in my pocket, fumbling awkwardly. I always carried lots of change, as it came in handy for my daily bus rides.

"Here you go." With a friendly smile that I hoped would invite further conversation, I offered her a dollar's worth of coins in exchange for a bill.

"Thanks." Her return smile radiated warmth. We made small talk for a couple of minutes.

"Where do you work?"

"What do you do there?"

"You're on K Street? Have you discovered the K Street Eatery yet?"

"You just graduated from school? Me too!"

The conversation paused as the bus pulled up and opened its doors. I followed her up the steps into cool, air-conditioned comfort, wondering if we would be able to continue. There were a few single seats available, but no doubles. My heart sank just a little as I thought that this pleasant exchange, barely started, was about to abruptly end.

She kept walking down the aisle, passing all of the available single seats, until she reached the hard, unoccupied orange and blue seats that lined the bus's last row. There was room enough for five people. Delighted, I sat down next to her.

We had fifteen minutes of animated conversation, sharing details about our new jobs, recent school experiences, and favorite neighborhood spots. I was vaguely aware of the diesel fume smell emanating from the engine below and the fact that it was also warming our seats on a hot day. As we continued chatting, I was captivated, thinking, *She is so easy to talk to—so friendly, solicitous, and engaging. She is so attractive. And what a smile!* My mind raced as we talked. *How can I gracefully end this conversation when she gets off the bus so that I can see her again?*

It didn't quite occur to me that I would likely see her at the bus stop the very next day. No, I was sure that I had to come up with a clever "next step" conversation-ender.

"This is my stop. It was so nice to meet you, Art," she said, gathering her oversized work bag, slinging it over her shoulder, and getting up. I slid aside to let her out.

"It was nice to meet you too, Kate." And then I awkwardly asked, "By the way, where do you live?"

Her smile disappeared. *Shoot, did I just say that?* She assumed a distant look as she processed the question and pondered how to respond.

After another moment's hesitation, her smile returned, and she said, "I'm at 2410 37th Street, right by Wisconsin Avenue." My pulse quickened.

"I know where that is! It's right behind Bob's Famous, my favorite ice cream place. I'll swing by sometime and maybe we can get a treat."

"I love Bob's—that would be great." She was off, and my day brightened even more.

My professional life's start was less auspicious. The timing to begin a career at a federal regulatory agency could not have been worse. Ronald Reagan was elected president three months after I started, and his administration was working hard to dismantle federal regulatory programs. The EPA was high on its hit list, and predictably, the agency was gutted.

Months after the fall election, I had a do-nothing job. My lasting image of that time is of a department comprised of smart, young, highly motivated PhD economists and MBAs sitting around a conference room table chatting over bottomless cups of coffee and speculating about the coming agency-wide layoffs, while playing Scrabble or Monopoly. It was bizarre and disheartening.

It was also a valuable life lesson. My vision of serving the greater good through government employment, a value instilled by my Depression- and New Deal–era parents, ran into a wall called *reality*. It crumbled. *A career in government service is not such a great idea after all,* I thought, responding to the moment. My equally idealistic EPA colleagues, bored and becoming increasingly cynical, also longed to get out of government and get "real jobs" in the private sector.

After a wasted year at the EPA, I left for a position at a consulting firm. I vowed to never go back to a public service job unless I went in at an organization's top leadership role. Only then could I possibly have the power to dictate policy, strategy, and execution. The EPA experience was formative, and to a large extent it dissuaded me from engaging in a meaningful service career role for the next twenty-five years.

Meanwhile, Kate and I delighted in Washington's many cultural and outdoor offerings—trips to museums, strolls through parks, weekend getaways to the Appalachian foothills, and our favorite summertime leisure activity, hours-long *al fresco* dinners on her open-air front porch. Meals became events, both for the food and the conversation.

A year after that first bus stop meeting, as we jitterbugged in a DC ballroom, I proposed to Kate. Although I had been thinking about it for weeks, the timing was spur-of-the-moment. We both enjoyed swing dancing, and while I was swept up, I also knew it was right. With Duke Ellington's "Take the 'A' Train" in the background, I would later think it was meant to be that we'd end up in New York City. We married in 1982, exactly two years after we met.

We took frequent skiing trips in our early days together. Our skill levels were pretty basic, though I was slightly more advanced than her. We would ski separately in the mornings, both of us finding terrain to match our skills, and then we'd ski together in the afternoons on her choice of trails.

One day she said, "Art, I saw the trail you were skiing this morning, and I want to try it."

"Okay, but are you sure?" I responded, thinking that this steep and very bumpy trail was not a good idea for her.

"Yes, I want to try it," she confidently asserted.

"Okay." *Well, good for her to give it a go*, I thought.

We stared down from the top of the trail for a couple minutes, nervously contemplating the task ahead. Then off I went. I found my rhythm and was completely caught up in the moment's rush. I kept going for a couple hundred yards before stopping. It was a thrilling ride. I looked up to see how Kate was doing, hoping that she had followed me.

Nope. She hadn't moved. She was still standing at the top and looking down. *Uh oh, she is petrified*, I thought. *Poor Kate! I made a big mistake by agreeing to bring her here. She's probably going to be pissed at me too*. I continued to watch and wait. More minutes passed. *She's paralyzed with fear*. I knew that feeling, staring down, a steep pitch ahead, and terrified to push off. *Take your skis off and walk down*, I kept thinking. *It's okay*.

Then she skidded off the top—tentatively, slowly, carefully traversing the trail from one side to another, sliding just a little as she went, and making the barest amount of headway downhill. She slid to a stop at the end of her traverse, sat down, turned her skis in the opposite direction while still seated, and got up. She then repeated her slow traverse to the other side of the trail. Again, she slid to a stop, sat down, turned her skis while seated, and then stood up to prepare for her next traverse. She continued in this manner, traversing a couple dozen times, before finally nearing the end where I waited.

Watching her was excruciating. Whatever time had elapsed, probably around twenty minutes or more, it felt like an eternity. All the time I felt awful for the terrifying experience that she must be having. I prepared myself to deal with her anxiety, frustration, and anger.

As she finally approached the bottom and skied up to me, she was all smiles.

"Art, that was fabulous!" she gushed. "I love these moguls! I can do this! Let's do it again!"

As I got to know her better, this is one of the things that I've always loved about Kate. She has guts. A sense of adventure. She'll try anything. She willingly tests her limits, and if she has fears, as she occasionally does, she overcomes them. The only failure for Kate is in not trying. She takes this approach to everything—her work, her personal life, everything. I am inspired by her, and I often hope that her can-do spirit will rub off on me. What a refreshing counterpoint to my own risk-averse, fear-of-failing instincts.

Kate received her master's degree two years after we married, and we were game for a major lifestyle change. When she landed a promising offer in New York, it was good timing for me to reboot my career and try something completely new. New York City's financial services industry stoked my curiosity, appealing to my analytical, problem-solving side. I was also alienated by Washington's political climate, as my earlier vision of a DC-based public service career was long since turned upside down. We were ambitious twenty-somethings, nervously excited to begin new phases of our careers and a new life together in a faster-paced world that offered greater opportunities. We began working in New York City on the same summer day in 1984, she at a management consulting firm, and me at American Express Company.

Her work ethic was indomitable. It was to a great extent shaped by difficult childhood experiences. As the only child of a struggling single mom, Kate became highly self-reliant. She eventually put herself through Georgetown University with a combination of financial aid and part-time work, holding up to three jobs simultaneously while in college. She received little help from family.

Achieving financial security, although she rarely talked about it, was a primary motivating factor behind her tireless drive. She was not materialistic, but she had a deep-seated fear of being poor. That was influenced by her childhood experience, notably from observing her mother's difficulties in making ends meet.

She combined her professional ambition with an instinctive connection to community. She empathized with people who struggled, particularly children from poor families who were falling behind in school, or who otherwise led troubled lives. Kate always found time to volunteer, and supporting education for the less fortunate was her primary focus. At her urging, we spent many an hour in those early days tutoring kids in the Washington, DC, schools. Her adventurous spirit, work ethic, and dedication to community—all wrapped in a kind, generous heart—have always inspired my unabashed admiration.

Of course, there were many things we did not see eye to eye on too. A big one was finances, and it took me awhile to realize how differently we thought about our needs. In contrast to Kate, I did not experience hardship growing up. I took it as a matter of faith that we would always make enough to support a family—perhaps not luxuriously, but more than adequately. A middle-class lifestyle was perfectly fine—I didn't need or want more. These were my Depression-era parents' utilitarian values speaking. All we needed was enough to cover basic lifestyle needs and an occasional nice vacation, or so I thought.

As Kate and I experienced how quickly two seemingly good salaries were consumed in a high-priced place like New York City, my perspective shifted and hers was affirmed. Four years after our move to New York, with its high cost of living and the large student-debt burden we carried, we still had no savings. I couldn't imagine how we would ever afford even a small down payment on a house, let alone start a family someday. Reality threw cold water on my belief that the money part of my life would take care of itself as long as I just found a good job and worked hard. This wasn't New London in the 1960s, or even Washington, DC, in the early 1980s. My inner pragmatist took over. We buckled down and eliminated all discretionary spending, right down to our $12 magazine subscriptions, in order to save money.

When our first child, Max, was born several years later in 1993, we scraped together a down payment and bought a house in suburban New Jersey, taking on a scarily large mortgage. A few years later, when Kate had a difficult pregnancy with our second child, Elena, she could no longer work. The stakes were raised one more time as financially we became fully dependent on me and my career success. I was prepared, but I also felt added pressure as the sole financial provider for a growing family.

Another key factor influencing my evolving money attitude came directly from my American Express experience. As my career steadily progressed, I was surprised at how well the company paid its most senior people. In the process of becoming one of them, being well paid gradually transformed from hope, to want, to need, and finally to expectation. The form of compensation, too, caused my thinking to further change. My salary, while continuing to increase, became a smaller percentage of my overall compensation. The company dangled big paydays before us in the form of deferred stock options, but they were ours to keep only if we stayed with the company for years to come. It got to the point where there was a great deal of wealth to be gained through continued company employment, but *only* through continued company employment. That structure, by design, caused many of us to make long-term company commitments, as the incentives for staying employed there just kept growing.

The value of those future paydays was seductive. That, in conjunction with our family's increasing needs and a high level of job satisfaction, made committing to a career at American Express an easy decision. It felt, in terms of career, like I had everything I could reasonably hope for—a satisfying, well-paying job with a future at a high-quality company. I didn't have as much time as I wanted for Kate or our children, and I didn't otherwise have a personal life, but I rationalized that that was the price to pay. I knew my role.

The idealistic vision I had as a young, Washington, DC–based professional nearly two decades earlier, as well as the plan for an even-handed life that balanced work with enriching leisure activities—family, friends, culture, sports—were distant memories. My inner pragmatist was now in control. By the time I reached middle age, I was fully bought in to a conventional lifestyle formula and on a low-resistance path: a steady, well-paying corporate career with one company; a nice suburban home; a long commute; a young, growing family with a stay-at-home wife who minded the home front; and a willingness to be the sole financial provider.

I was grateful for my good fortune as I commuted to work on 9/11.

PART III

Art in the Middle Ages

9

THE TWILIGHT ZONE

What does not kill me
makes me stronger.
—Friedrich Nietzsche

August, 2003.

I embrace my new lateral-but-really-a-demotion job at American Express's Minneapolis subsidiary with a positive attitude. At least I try; I have to. It's the only way to buy time and figure out what to do next. I also grudgingly come to grips with a new reality—after nearly twenty years with the company, the advancement stage of my American Express career is over. Questions about my next steps are constantly top-of-mind, and satisfying answers elude me. Now approaching my late forties, I enter an uncomfortable muddling-through phase with no clear forward path.

When I work through difficult periods, I sometimes draw metaphorical parallels to running a marathon. Having run a few as a younger man, I know that maintaining a strong, steady pace for an extended period is the key to success. It's extraordinarily difficult. Marathoners need to expend high energy, maintain focus, overcome obstacles, stay patient, and, most of all, persist. If successful, they will sustain that strong, steady pace while always keeping an eye on the prize—the finish line. The physical challenges are great, but the mental and emotional challenges can be greater. Marathoners constantly play mental games to cope with adversity, stay focused, and recalibrate as needed.

The marathon I now imagine myself running is no ordinary race. I liken it to a scenario from *The Twilight Zone*, a 1960s television show known for its creepy reality distortions and Kafkaesque scenes and plots. *The Twilight Zone* marathon I'm picturing has no course markers and no finish line. Participating in *The Twilight Zone* marathon, I continuously run but don't make progress. Still, I keep running, convinced that it's the only way through, looking for signs and seeing none. I relentlessly push my physical and emotional limits, hoping that at some point course markers and ultimately a finish line will magically appear.

Course markers are critical for maintaining a marathoner's pacing plan. They are opportunities to ask important questions: How am I feeling? Does this feel right at this stage? Am I on track? Do I need to modify my plan? How? These checkpoints are needed for ongoing adjustments, whether it's fine-tuning or a major reset. Importantly, they also allow runners to manage their expectations for the remaining miles to the finish. During a race, a marathoner's brain is in overdrive.

As I imagine running *The Twilight Zone* marathon and not seeing mile markers or other checkpoints, I do not know when, how, or if the race will end. All I know is that if I slow down, I will fall behind and never catch up. I persist, not letting up for a minute, searching and hoping that I will find some way to measure progress. *How many miles to the finish? Is there a finish line?* It is mentally exhausting.

"Art, I think you need some help," observes Bob, one year after the organizational change that altered my career trajectory. "You're in a rut. You need some help," he repeats, surprising me with this observation.

I hesitate for a couple seconds as I contemplate an appropriate response while also cynically wondering what's really motivating the comment. I silently concede the point with a full body shrug. *He's right, but where is this leading?* I warily wait for him to continue.

"I think that you need an executive coach," he asserts confidently. "We'll pay for it."

"Hmm," I nod, pausing as I contemplate his suggestion. "That's a generous offer, and I like the idea, Bob, but I'd also like to give it some more thought."

Meanwhile, I continue wondering, *What's really going on here?* I decide to go forward with it. *I could certainly use some help,* I think. *Maybe I do need a coach.*

I interview a few coaches, and I particularly like Raymond. "I understand your situation, Art. I'm not a typical coach. I focus on purpose, values, and motivation. I'll help you figure out how these factors, combined with your professional style, best align with Financial Advisors' culture. When you can match your purpose and style, your career goals, and your company's behavioral norms, you'll have the best outcome. I sense that you've got a disconnect. I can help you sort that out."

Raymond has written extensively on living life with purpose and breaking down personal, emotional barriers in order to achieve greater satisfaction and success. This bigger picture perspective is precisely what I want. At this point, I am steeped in negativity and unable to see a path forward. I have continued to stubbornly persist, even as the race-with-no-end is taking a heavy emotional toll.

I need a professional shrink, and in Raymond I find one. Leaving my twenty-year employer is increasingly likely. My rational side knows that, but emotionally I struggle with the idea. Deep down, I wonder if leaving would be a sign of surrender. My inability to develop a satisfying "what's next" vision is also giving me pause. I cannot figure this out on my own.

Raymond is late middle-aged, medium height, and has a thin frame and a receding, graying hairline. He has a professorial air. This belies his intense, no-nonsense bearing, which is accentuated by his piercing stare when making a point.

Raymond forces me to make hard-headed assessments, to face up to what really matters, and to better prioritize. I quickly face what I've known in my gut but have lacked the courage and humility to accept—that being at American Express is a style and values mismatch. I wanted to think that it was temporary—that I could crack the code and overcome it, or at least outlast it. I wanted to view it as a test, one that I could meet head-on and pass. I wanted to view it as if I had just hit a difficult patch in a marathon, one that I could work through by simply persisting.

"Art, don't you get it?" Raymond implores with a raised voice, his eyes aflame and boring into mine. "You are not well-suited for this place. This organizational culture is a star system; it's self-promotional; it's ego-driven. That's the way it is. It works for some people, but it's not for you. This is reality. It's about chemistry and fit, not about quality."

"What are you saying? That I can't succeed here?" I ask, still stubbornly unwilling to concede the point.

"It depends on how you define success. By some measures you're succeeding, but at what cost? You feel undervalued. You feel stuck. Is this the kind of place you want to be? You're more effective in a culture based on collaboration and trust. You're a team player. You're a servant-style leader. That's who you are. Think about where you've succeeded in the past. You value relationships and teamwork. Those qualities are not priorities here. Sure, you can keep muddling through, but that's never going to feel good. It doesn't mean you failed; it means that this is not a good place for you."

I know I am out of place, yet until now I've clung to the irrational hope that I could buy time and eventually sort it out. *Try harder. Work smarter. Problem-solve better.* I never acknowledged that I could be wrong. The idea of leaving before exhausting every possibility had felt like giving up. I finally accept that the problem is staring at me in the mirror, and I need to own it. It's time to wake up, recognize reality, set pride aside, and cut my losses.

There are other more personal issues that bother me too. My life is severely out of balance. Since moving to the Twin Cities, I've allowed work to take over my life. I work, and then I engage with my family with whatever little time and energy I have left. I have few interests or friends outside of work.

I often arrive home late in the evening, after our children have gone to bed. I go into their bedrooms to see each one sleeping. On these days, just seeing them, even if for a minute, is my only way for connection. It warms my heart. It also saddens me, knowing I've completely missed another day in their lives, time that is forever lost.

I had many professional colleagues from my New York days who rarely saw their children during the week because of long working hours and difficult commutes. They rationalized that this was normal, as many grew up in the area and had similar experiences as children—they rarely saw their fathers during the work week. Thankfully, that was not my experience. I told myself I would never become that dad, and that if it occasionally happened, I would never allow it to become the norm.

My September 11th experience is always in the back of my mind too. I carry graphic mental images of people through a black smoky haze, sitting on the ledge of the World Trade Center's ninety-third floor moments before their deaths. It haunts me. These were ordinary professionals, just like me, doing their jobs one minute, and the next minute they had a death sentence. I start to think, *If my life ended tomorrow, would I look back and be satisfied with the choices I made?*

Raymond encourages me to develop a personal mission statement in order to focus my thinking. My personal mission is to use my skills and experience to help others. That starts with my family but also includes friends and community members, especially those community members who do not have the good fortune and privilege that I have. This aligns with my core personal values, the values I learned from my parents, and values that Kate practices daily. I have no idea how to connect this personal mission to my career, but it's a start.

It's now inescapably clear that I have to leave American Express, and sooner rather than later. I don't have a clear next step, and that had paralyzed me, but not anymore. That uncertainty feels unimportant now. It's hard to understand how deeply locked in I have been to a narrow way of thinking. As I become more self-aware, and with a lot of help, I start planning for my post–American Express future. It's early 2005, two-and-a-half years after our Minneapolis move. I finally have clarity. No more muddling through; I am ready to leave my personal *Twilight Zone*.

Then life intervenes, and everything changes.

10

THE PERFECT JOB

There comes the strangest moment in your life,
when everything you thought before breaks free—
what you relied upon, as ground-rule and as rite
looks upside down from what it used to be.
—Kate Light, "There Comes the
Strangest Moment"

There is a commotion as I approach my building's foyer early
one morning. People from the company's public relations department and a few senior leaders are aggressively handing
out flyers to all arriving staff. I've not seen anything like this before.
Something is amiss.

"What's up, Michelle?" I ask one of my colleagues, who is handing out what looks like a press release.

She turns, smiles, walks over, and thrusts a printed page into my
hand. "Art, you won't believe this!" she exclaims. "American Express is
getting rid of us!" She rolls her eyes and nervously laughs.

"What? What are you talking about?"

"I know, I can't believe it myself! American Express is going to
spin us off."

"What?"

"There's going to be an IPO for Financial Advisors. We're going to
be an independent company."

"Are you kidding? How did this happen? What does it mean? Do you know any more about it?"

"No, I just heard this morning! I heard that even Jay (our CEO) didn't know. Everyone's in a state of shock!"

I enter the building and head toward the elevator bank, lost in thought as I process this new information.

American Express's plan to spin off Financial Advisors surprises everyone, including leadership. Jay and Bob, our two most senior leaders, were unaware of a plan that was hatched by the New York–based parent company.

Overnight, Financial Advisors has a monumental and unexpected set of to-dos. Within a few short months, we will have to execute a $10 billion initial public offering to launch a new public company that will become Ameriprise Financial. We are figuring out how to do this on the fly. It is an all-hands-on-deck event, and there is a dramatic, instantaneous change in the environment.

A number of new positions are created to help kick-start this process. I am appointed to one of them: corporate treasurer for the soon-to-be-created company. I had long aspired to be a company treasurer, though I couldn't see a path at American Express. A treasurer position is much better aligned with my skills and experience than the CFO job I unsuccessfully auditioned for a couple years earlier. In a flash, my career has new life. Just like that, it goes from dead-end to the perfect job. *Whoa!* I feel grateful and determined to make the most of it. My thoughts about leaving the company immediately move to the back burner. I approach work with renewed energy and excitement; it feels great.

It feels great, that is, until it doesn't. The initial injection of positive energy wears off quickly. The perfect job, I learn, may exist on paper, but I cannot escape reality. There are a lot of reasons why I dislike working here, and virtually all of them are still present. With the building pressure of a looming transactional deadline, the workplace culture deteriorates even further.

I do my best to block out the negatives and to focus simply on getting the job done. It is the best of times and the worst of times for me, and that is hard to process. While I appreciate the professional opportunity, I realize yet again that I am still not a good fit for this company. My chronic disappointment and cynicism come roaring back within months.

"Hey, Ron! It's so great to see you!" I say, all smiles, as I bounce up from my table with genuine delight to greet him. Ron is a former New York–based American Express colleague who is now at J.P. Morgan, one of the country's most prestigious financial institutions. I am in New York on other business, and I take the opportunity to meet him for dinner. My goal is to convince him to relocate to Minneapolis and join my fledgling treasury team. If I am successful, he will be a perfect fit for my team's most critical needs.

We are in a noisy Midtown restaurant, and it has an unmistakable urban, midweek bustle. It's not the best setting for this conversation, but it will do. The lights are a little dim, and unlike many New York City eateries, there is ample room between tables for a quasi-private conversation. We both eagerly order wine as we get the dialog off to a jaunty start. We do a quick, obligatory check-in of jobs and families, and then we get down to business.

"Ron, this whole IPO thing is very exciting," I start, reflecting the positivity I am genuinely feeling at this moment. The wine is helping. "It's uncharted territory for us, and it's a fabulous opportunity to have an impact. I've got so much to do, trying to figure out the right capital structure, lining up the bankers, getting our subsidiaries rated—it's a long list. It's kind of freaking me out, but it's fun. This is exactly the role I've always wanted. And an urgent challenge right now is to build my team . . ." I go on and on. I am in full-blown sales mode, and I make it very clear I want to recruit him as a key team member.

We both lean forward as I speak. He is nodding with every point, and his eyes sparkle with anticipation. *I think I've got him.*

"That all sounds great, Art. Tell me, too, about Minneapolis as a place to live. What was it like to relocate your family from the New York area?"

"It's great, Ron. Minneapolis has all the advantages of a big city without the negatives. It's got great theater, a world-class orchestra, good schools, restaurants, professional sports; it really has it all."

Continuing to sell as I set the hook deeper, I feel a creeping sense of discomfort. It takes over my mind, and then my body. Shifting in my seat, I deliberately slow down my presentation and consciously lean back, my mind racing as I second-guess the entire purpose of this conversation.

What am I doing? Ron is a good guy. Why am I trying to sell him on joining a company that I dislike? Can I ask him to relocate his entire family for this? He'll probably end up knowing he made a big mistake, just like me.

I keep talking but deliberately tone it down, substituting a matter-of-fact presentation for my self-consciously promotional sales pitch. I'm now overcome with ambivalence, and I don't know where to take this conversation. "For all of those good things, Ron, in fairness, you need to know about some of the potential downsides. You need to consider this with eyes wide open."

He slowly sits back, contemplating my words and changed tone. He gets the unspoken message, and we struggle to maintain eye contact. He continues to pepper me with questions, and they become more critically probing. The powerful excitement we both felt, present just fifteen minutes earlier, completely evaporates.

Our dinner is cordial to the end. "Congratulations, Art, on being in such a great spot. I'll think about our conversation and get back to you," he says. "It sounds like a wonderful opportunity." He smiles warmly as he leaves.

Despite his positive parting words, his body language communicated a different message: he won't take the job. I feel relieved. *What's my problem? Here I am, trying to build my team, and I can't in good conscience ask a high-quality guy to join?*

Six months into the perfect job, I am deeply dissatisfied, and it strikes me like a gut punch. My job, on its face, is alluring. It has all the trappings of success—position, title, prestige, influence, and generous compensation. It represents something else that is important to me—personal redemption. I like the idea of being the company's treasurer, and I have to admit the ego gratification feels good. The day-to-day is another story completely. *What am I going to do?* I'm not sure.

I never understood the concept of burnout. I always wondered if it was an excuse, a way of rationalizing failure, of justifying quitting. Privately, that's what I had thought. Now I know better.

I am deep into it, and I am ready to be done. The perfect job, on the surface, has everything I long coveted and worked hard for, yet I intensely dislike it. As my executive coach, Raymond, memorably observed, "You can't fake engagement." I now realize I've been doing that for too long, and I am worn out. Another friend's words, taken from a different context, come to mind: "I'm sick and tired of being sick and tired."

The implications are not that complicated—I should leave. Although, once again, convincing myself of this is difficult. I am also struggling with another, more difficult question: *even if I convince myself leaving is the best next step, do I have the guts to do it?*

I still struggle with the lingering thought that leaving is tantamount to quitting; that it represents failure. Intellectually, I know otherwise, but I am fighting a lifetime of socialization about what constitutes success and failure; about the value of persistence—I've learned to never give up. My ego and identity are wrapped up in this role too. I am wrestling with that, even as my rational instincts tell me that resigning is the right thing to do. I'm coming around but am not there yet.

I make up excuses to stay: with three children, private school tuition, and college tuitions looming, our family needs the money; no one just gets up and leaves a job like this—that would be irresponsible; I don't have another job waiting, and it will take some time to find something else suitable, so I can't leave yet; it's an irreversible decision, so if I don't resign today, I still have the option to do it tomorrow; and on and on. There's a steady stream of excuses for inaction, and I use them all to affirm my self-inflicted paralysis.

Meanwhile, the reasons for leaving are piling up too. Kate is encouraging me to leave. She has seen me through all of the emotional ups and downs. She knows that the chronic insomnia I developed when we moved to Minneapolis is due to work-related stress, and that's now getting worse. She knows no job is worth the emotional price we are paying as a family. She wants her husband back—healthier, happier, and physically and emotionally more present at home. She wants this for me as much as for herself, and she is more than willing to support me interrupting my career to regain normalcy.

Finally, one of the most important lessons of 9/11, that every day is a precious gift to be savored, is on my mind. I feel trapped, and I want to feel good again. That won't happen until I leave.

It strikes me as odd. After a steady, two-decade ascent to reach the perfect job, and after being in this role for just a short time, it now feels unimportant. I don't value it, and I don't want it. My life is misaligned in ways I struggle to articulate. I know what has to be done but still can't bring myself to do it. Postponing action is the path of least resistance. Bold was never my style, and now a lack of courage is holding me back.

While I dither, external circumstances take over and force the issue. I'm finding it harder to focus. I can feel my job performance slipping, and it's frustrating. But I am also caring less. My relationship with Bob steadily deteriorates, and contentious interactions are now more commonplace. After one of these exchanges, he angrily challenges me, "Art, this isn't working! What's going on with you?"

The room is silent. It's the right question—I have certainly not been at my best—but I immediately and defensively focus on his accusatory tone. It triggers me. My pent-up frustrations weigh heavily. There is a long, awkward pause, as I try to control my emotions before responding. Searching silently for the right words and tone, I am at a loss.

Then, more calmly, he asks, "What are you going to do?"

Understanding exactly what he's asking, I know the time has come. "Give me the night to sleep on it, Bob, and let's talk in the morning." I want to make sure I get this right.

The next morning, I go to his office first thing. I sit down, look him in the eye, and say, "It's time for me to go." He looks away. Staring down at his desk, he quietly says, "Okay." I sense that he is enormously relieved. My response spares him the trouble of dealing with a long-tenured, high-profile employee who is checked out.

We continue the conversation, immediately getting tactical about the terms of separation. He is gracious and generous, and we quickly reach agreement. Among other things, I will stay on for another three months to assure a smooth transition. I will leave in August 2006, four years after I began in Minneapolis. This career chapter will end just before my fiftieth birthday.

In the following weeks, I have many conversations with company colleagues about my leaving. It surprises me that the first thing many do is compliment me on having the courage to resign. Their perception is that I stood on principle, am leaving a bad situation, and am showing courage by walking away from a high-visibility leadership role and the generous compensation that comes with it.

I appreciate their supportive sentiments, though I see it differently. This was a bad fit from the start. I'd persisted, despite my unhappiness, for a long time. I ignored reality and vainly thought I could make it work until near the end. Bob's challenging question had forced the issue, and resigning was the only rational response. That was an overdue acceptance of reality; it was not a courageous act.

No matter. I'm leaving, and it's for the best.

11

REFLECTION

Along and unhappy chapter ended the day I resigned from Ameriprise. It's hard to fathom in retrospect, but at the age of forty-nine, I barely remembered there was much more to life than the narrow view from inside my corporate bubble. That recognition would take time to form. I was not prepared to give up on my business-focused ambitions—not yet—but I was ready to both rediscover and learn anew what else the world had to offer.

A weight lifted, and I felt optimistic for the first time in a long time. While disappointed over the whole Minneapolis experience, I had no regrets and no ill will. I was thankful for my opportunities and especially thankful for my greater gifts: a supportive, intact family; good health; experience gained from a lengthy corporate career; and financial security. I was lucky; I had good fortune that many did not.

I began to see things differently. New, enduring perspectives were emerging within me. The first were backward-looking, calling out and rejecting old ways of thinking: I would no longer uncritically follow conventional paths, allowing others to set the course and establish the rules of the road; I would not measure success according to others' judgments; I would not define myself by a job or even a profession; I would shed my blinders and openly embrace wider-ranging possibilities; and I would not allow mindless persistence and pride to drive my decisions.

My first priority was very simple—I needed a break—time to breathe, time to reconnect with my family, and time to regain perspective. With a little bit of time, I realized that I wanted more. Much more.

It was time to simplify—to let life happen in a more natural, less deterministic way and to reconnect with my core values. My corporate career had to crash before any of that could happen.

12

ONE-WAY TICKETS

Oh the Places You'll Go!
—Book by Dr. Seuss

The company pretty much leaves me alone during my three-month on-site transition period. *Okay, I have the gift of time. How can I make the most of it?* Self-criticism sets right in and distracts me. I keep replaying my experiences, looking for answers. *Why did I let it go for so long? Fear of the unknown?* Yes. *A reflexive persistence, fueled by an unwillingness to accept reality?* For sure. These are honest, albeit unsatisfying, answers. Whatever. I need to learn from this, but mostly I need to think prospectively—how to best get on with my life.

Mike Tyson once said, "Everyone has a good plan until he gets punched in the face." That resonates. I had a good plan when we moved to Minnesota four years ago. Then I took a punch in the face.

I'm about to turn fifty years old and become unemployed. Always the responsible provider, my focus now turns to finding my next job. I'll use this time to start looking. It won't be hard—*I am in the right business, the right function, and have the right experience. I'm at the wrong company. It's that simple—just a bad fit. It will work out much better somewhere else.* At least, that's what my closest colleagues and executive coach are advising me, and I agree. Follow the sensible, conventional path; that's the rational thing to do. I craft a thoughtful Plan A and expect an easy transition.

The plan quickly dissolves in waves of uncharacteristically fresh thinking. It just feels wrong. I am looking for something else but cannot figure out what or why. I start to think that maybe the best plan is to not have a plan.

I'm perplexed but also curious where things might go if I set aside career-planning thoughts and begin considering a wider range of possibilities. It feels good to regain a sense of control and that all-important ingredient for positive thinking—hope. I start to explore less-conventional paths.

I also vow to not waste time looking back with thoughts of "would have," "should have," or "why didn't I." I am doing my best to put self-doubt and negativity behind me.

"What's done is done," Mom often said.

I make two decisions that will be life-changing, although at the time, I have no inkling of their impact. First, I commit to run a marathon. I think that it will help to focus my energy, settle my emotions, and improve my physical health. It will also challenge me and give me a sense of accomplishment. I need all of those things.

My initiation to recreational running, over three decades earlier, was inauspicious. At the age of seventeen, I entered a twelve-mile road race on my brother's dare, three days before it was held. This was the early 1970s, well before recreational jogging was a thing. I'd never run more than a mile before, and I didn't have a clue. I didn't train a single day. *What could be so hard about putting one foot in front of the other, and then repeating?*

It was a hot, sunny August afternoon as I toed the start line in my high-top Chuck Taylors and floppy wool socks. I had no understanding of pacing and started way too fast. It didn't take long for me to flame out. Four miles in, hyperventilating and consumed by heat exhaustion, I thought I was going to die. I gasped for breath, stepped off the course, and bent over, hands on my knees, and heaved. I found a shady patch of grass along the side of the road and lay down for a few minutes. I eventually got up, decided to continue, and tagged along with a bunch of younger boys who were intermittently walking and jogging. I finished 159th out of 172 runners. Exhausted and humbled, I vowed to never run again.

The painful emotional hangover lasted many years. But once I started working for a living, I had to do something to stay physically active, and a daily jog met my needs. Those runs were surprisingly renewing, and they became integral to my new lifestyle.

Running a marathon is a whole different level of commitment. This would not be my first marathon, but it would be the first in a long time.

It's August 1986, and I'm thirty years old. I met Tony, an off-duty police officer, just a few hours earlier. We are on a daylong group bicycle ride in New York City. We learn that running is a common interest, and we make a good connection. I proudly share that I have run many 10Ks.

"Someday I'd like to try a marathon," I say, not sure if I believe it. The 10K distance is challenging enough. But giving voice to whimsical stretch goals is something I occasionally do. I will openly share these goals, as if by saying them to others, I'll be more likely to act on them. The idea of running a marathon is more of a curiosity than a goal. I have no conscious desire, and certainly no plan, to try to run one.

Then Tony surprises me.

"I've got an entry for this year's race," Tony discloses, referring to the New York City Marathon. "I won't be able to run it. I want you to have it, Art. Do you want it?" he offers with a kind smile.

It's an incredibly generous offer, and it catches me completely off guard. I immediately, instinctively, and enthusiastically say yes. It's ridiculous for me to accept this offer. The marathon is in twelve weeks, and I can't possibly prepare for a marathon in such a short period of time. Yet as soon as I say it, I know that I'll do it. There will be no backing down.

The next day, I get Bob Glover's *The Competitive Runner's Handbook*. It's the closest thing to a runner's bible, and I devour its advice. I commit to succeed—or at least to avoid a disaster—and with a short training window, I go for it. Motivated by both fear and excitement, I train hard seven days a week right to the end. It nearly kills me. It also starts to take hold, as I feel my body changing in a good way. The roots of my future running obsession, for the first time, find fertile ground and sprout.

On weekend training runs in Central Park, I often observe a large contingent of disabled athletes, members of Achilles International, who are also preparing for the marathon. I see one of the athletes featured on *Sixty Minutes,* the national television news show. She trains every Saturday morning. She has cerebral palsy and uses handheld crutches to propel herself. I am in awe seeing these disabled athletes slowly circling the park, training for hours. I am inspired, and even as I am chronically tired and sore, I remind myself to never again complain about my own aches and pains.

On the day of the race, I feel ready. Unfortunately, despite having read the runner's bible and trained hard, I make classic rookie mistakes. I don't properly hydrate. I don't pace myself well. I develop acute pain in both knees at around the halfway mark, and I don't know what to do. I think back to my training book and recall guidance that says if you have pain in one knee and not the other, then you've got a problem. But if you have pain in both knees, that could just be normal fatigue or wear and tear.

OK, so do I just suck it up and keep going? The pain is intense and worsening. *Can this possibly be normal?* I can't imagine. At mile twenty, I am running over the bridge from Manhattan to the Bronx, and I look down through the metal grate at the Harlem River's rocky shoals one hundred feet below. Miserable, I think, *I can just jump now and end the pain, or I can keep going and bear it for another six miles.*

Nearly an hour later, stumbling across the finish line, my race is over and the physical pain finally subsides. I don't feel proud. I feel wasted and let down. After training hard and expecting I-don't-know-what, something much better than this, I am an empty vessel. I am also mystified. *Why do people do this? What an awful experience!* I no longer have any curiosity about running a marathon.

Four days later, the final Achilles athlete crosses the finish line in a time of ninety-eight hours. He is a forty-year-old double amputee, a Vietnam veteran named Bob Wieland. He traveled the twenty-six-mile course by leaning forward, planting his hands on the ground, and swinging his body to propel it, landing upright on his legless torso. He would then lean forward again, repeating the swinging motion. He covered several miles a day doing this, stopping at each day's end to sleep, and then starting up the next morning from the prior day's end point. In an interview after the race, he said, "I may have lost my legs, but I didn't lose my heart."

This story amazes me. I cannot stop thinking about the other disabled athletes who train in Central Park, and another seed is planted. I could not have known then, but exactly thirty years later, I would be a volunteer support guide for an Achilles athlete, and we would set a New York City Marathon record.

The knee pain I experienced during the marathon was due to acute tendonitis. It's serious enough to sideline me for six months. Thankfully, the disappointment and painful memories start to fade with time. I get back to running 10Ks and even begin to think of giving marathoning another chance. I decide to try again five years later, in 1991, at the age of thirty-five.

Memories of my first marathon experience gnaw at me and are motivating. I still think about the pain and misery. Is it possible to run a marathon and finish feeling good? I don't know, and I want to find out. That's my goal: to finish and feel good. I also set a time target, but I decide that time doesn't really matter if it requires intense misery to achieve it. It's not that important. That doesn't mean I will run slowly. It means pushing myself to my limits and *still* feeling strong. That's what success will be. *Can I do this?*

It's a perfect running day—slight cloud cover, a cool temperature, and a light breeze—as I turn the corner at mile twenty-three from

Fifth Avenue into Central Park. I pass swelling crowds, lined three and four people deep on both sides. Their loud, intense screams of encouragement pierce the fragrant fall air, made even more aromatic by the smell of roasting chestnuts. *Only in New York.* There is a constant festive clanging of cow bells.

"Only three miles to go!"

"You've got this!"

"Woo hoo! Looking good!"

"Hey, it's Art! Go, Art!" I glance over my shoulder and catch an excited wave and smile from an American Express colleague. I enthusiastically toss a big wave and smile back.

As I head south on Park Drive, I am running down a wide, tree-lined avenue, and am greeted by a magnificent tapestry of gently falling leaves—reds, yellows, oranges, and a multitude of shades in between. The airborne leaves, softly swaying on their zigzagging path toward earth, blanket the air in front of me. It looks surreal, as the physical intensity of a marathon's late stages and the large, noisy crowds are juxtaposed against a magically fuzzy, Impressionistic foreground of soft, autumnal, earth-toned color.

I assess the three-mile distance to the finish against my energy level. *I can't believe it, but I've got this! I nailed it!* I am one hundred percent confident to reach what I thought was an impossible goal. *My God, do I feel good!* I become choked up and tears start streaming down my face. *Where is this coming from?* The struggle and long-standing disappointment from my last marathon attempt are melting in a puddle of tears. I didn't think this was possible. I kick it up another gear and steadily increase my pace to the end. My final mile is my fastest, and my overall time will be my lifetime personal best.

I reflect on these distant marathon memories as I transition out of Ameriprise. I consider the many reasons that attempting another marathon will be good for me. Now nearly fifty years old, I am also skeptical. *Am I too old for this? I can't fool Mother Nature, can I?*

Kate once again provides inspiration. She started long-distance running after we moved to Minnesota four years earlier, and it transformed her by helping her to conquer social isolation and the long Minnesota winters. She completed several marathons over those years, achieving a high level of fitness while also connecting to a great runners' friend network. When she competed, I would jump in and accompany her for the races' later stages. The positive vibes and the runners' can-do spirits were energizing.

I'm going for it.

I immerse myself in training and experience a new perspective on the therapeutic value of solo long runs. Long-distance runners often joke that running saves them the expense of paying a therapist. I learn why this is true. It had not occurred to me earlier in my life, as I usually had a running partner. But now is a different time. I go for many solo runs of up to three hours long, reflecting on my professional challenges and lessons learned. I start ruminating about my future, allowing my thoughts to wander unconstrained. I never know where they will take me, and that feels good. I also embrace the physicality of the experience—it fills me with energy and is personally empowering. My forty-nine-year-old body responds well.

The training process culminates with my running the 2006 Grandma's Marathon in Duluth. I have a strong run, and we also make it a fun and celebratory family event. Two hours after completing the race, I am in our hotel swimming pool with my two daughters, Elena and Elizabeth, ages seven and four, splashing around and doing some water running to begin my recovery. I feel strong, accomplished, and overwhelmed.

In the weeks that follow, I know that something is fundamentally changed. With my days at Ameriprise about to end, I am looking ahead, committing to an activity and a lifestyle. Feeling confident and fit, I set a new lifetime goal. If I say it out loud and share it, I will commit to it. I will turn fifty in two months. I say it: *I will run fifty marathons after I turn fifty.* "Fifty after Fifty" is a new personal mantra.

The second life-changing decision I make, in addition to running a marathon, is more immediate, dramatic, and disruptive.

Contemplating my next career step, I initially create a plan for networking, building my career narrative, and selling myself to prospective employers. Then I begin to think, *What's the rush?* We had long ago booked a two-week vacation to Italy for the end of the summer. That is still our plan, and we are excited. Kate and I vacationed there before, and we loved it. I am certainly in the right frame of mind to get on an airplane and go someplace whimsical and fun. Then I think, *Why limit ourselves to two weeks?* After all, we only need to be back in time for the kids to begin school.

I reflect back nearly twenty years earlier, to the time Kate and I toured Pompeii. We had a chance conversation with an American couple on a year's sabbatical. They were seeing the world with their twelve-year-old son. We engaged the boy in conversation.

"How are you enjoying your trip, Mark? Do you have a favorite place or memory?" I asked.

"Oh yeah, I loved touring Russia," he enthusiastically replied. "St. Petersburg was my favorite. I never thought I'd like museums, but they were really great." He described his travel experiences in impressive detail.

Now we are thinking of our own children, their interests, and their ages. Max, our thirteen-year-old, has a great curiosity for the world and for history. Although the girls are much younger, they too are curious, good travelers, and always open to new experiences.

What a wonderful gift we could give our family. *Can we do this?*

Wait a minute. *Aren't I supposed to find a job?* That, after all, is my role. *What about the kids? They have to go to school.*

I start to think more freely. I will take some time off from my professional life. *Why not?* We know that we can make it work. As for the children, we decide that school is a non-issue. The kids can go to school anywhere, or maybe not at all. I think of Mark Twain's nugget of wisdom: "Don't let schooling get in the way of your education."

I hastily research the options, as we only have a few weeks to sort this out before the school year starts. We form a new plan. Kate and

I discuss it extensively, but we really don't have to. Whenever we ask ourselves the question *"why not?"* we have no good answers. A greater gift awaits, and it's there for the taking.

We commit to the plan. We will move to Florence, Italy, and we will do it in three weeks in order to get there at the beginning of the school year. It has everything we could hope for—a high-quality international school for our children, a place where we can all get a rich cultural experience, a storied history, physical beauty, incredible food and wine—we see little downside. It will be the perfect base for a family adventure and a refreshing break. The key tasks are to get the kids enrolled in school, find an apartment, and rebook our flights. They are all surprisingly easy to do.

What about my career's next steps? All in good time. I'll figure it out.

We are excited as the plan comes together. The kids will meet children from all over the world. Kate and I will go to school there as well and study the Italian language, Florence's Renaissance history, and local cuisine. It will be *la dolce vita*. The downside? My career planning will be put on hold indefinitely, or at least until I decide to get serious. *If that's the only downside, this is an easy call.* Our children don't know what to make of this, but as they observe our excitement, they warm up to the idea.

We book one-way tickets and board a plane for Florence on my fiftieth birthday, exactly three weeks after I left Ameriprise. I am back on my feet and literally flying forward. We don't know how long this trip will last, and it doesn't matter. I know that eventually I will return to my life as a corporate finance professional; after all, that's who I am, and that's what I do.

It turns out I will be wrong about that. My days of making safe, predictable choices are over.

13

QUINDICI VIA VERRAZZANO

Blue skies
Smiling at me
Nothing but blue skies
Do I see . . .
—Irving Berlin, "Blue Skies"

Our family's traveling mettle is put to the test within two hours of boarding our plane. Following a short flight to Chicago's O'Hare International Airport, we learn that our connecting Alitalia flight is cancelled. A mere 350 miles from home, we are already knocked off course.

"I'll wait in line," I say to Kate. "We have a long day ahead, so why don't you and the kids find a comfortable place to hang out."

"Thanks, Art. It might be best to let them run around and burn some energy."

"Yeah, good idea."

I take my place in line to rebook. As I stare at the backs of twenty-five people in a line that isn't moving, I can feel my blood pressure rising.

"Dad, what happened?" seven-year-old Elena asks.

"Our flight was cancelled," I flatly reply, silently seething, and peevishly wondering why there is only one travel agent helping this long line of people. *And why is it so damned hot in here?*

"Why did they do that?"

"I don't know, dear."

"Does that mean we can't go to Italy?"

"Oh no, we're going, we'll just get there a little later," I say, smiling and willing myself into a calmer state.

"How are we going to get there if our flight was cancelled?"

"We have to get onto a different flight. That's why I'm waiting in this line. Don't worry, dear, we just have to be patient and it will work out."

"Okay," she smiles. "I'm going to go play with Lizzie. This airport is fun!" And she speeds off, racing down a wide concourse in pursuit of her sister.

Okay, we're on Italy time now. If we get there a day late, who the hell cares? It's all part of the adventure. Watching my kids joyfully play tag, I feel the tension drain from my neck and shoulders, and I patiently wait.

Six hours later, we are Frankfurt-bound on an Air India flight. We'll layover there for a couple hours and then get a connection to Florence. We are settled in, and Max, sitting behind me, leans forward and says in an urgent, loud whisper, "Dad, this is so cool! We're having *lamb curry* for dinner. Whoever heard of having lamb curry on an airplane?"

Two hours later, he taps my shoulder and says, "Dad, why are we going to Germany?" He pauses, then excitedly adds, "I've never been to Germany before."

"It's because our flight got cancelled. They put us on another flight so we can eventually get to Florence. It's just a different route that happens to go through Frankfurt."

"Do we have to pay extra?"

"No."

"Really?"

"Yes, that's how these things work when your flight is cancelled."

"You mean we get to go to Germany for *free*?"

"Yup!" I say, smiling.

"Oh my God, Dad, that is so awesome!" he cries, settling back in his seat to contemplate our great luck to spend two hours in Frankfurt's airport terminal.

We arrive in Florence midafternoon on a warm, bright late-summer day. Two of our suitcases don't make it; they will arrive five days later. We learn that is normal. ("Only two? You were lucky. This is Italy, you know," our landlord later remarked.) Not that any of that matters. Between five of us and the surviving suitcases, we load up two taxis for the short ride to our apartment.

"*Quindici via Verrazzano*," I confidently tell the taxi driver. 15 Verrazzano Street. I pronounce the street name "Ve-ra-*zah*-no" in my flat American accent. I lived in New York for years—I know how to pronounce Verrazzano.

"*Dove?*" ("Where?")

"Quindici via Verrazzano!"

"*Dove?*" His brow furrows more deeply.

"Quindici via Verrazzano!" I say slowly and loudly, as if that will help, but not knowing what else to do. I feel exasperated, and I dig into my wallet to confirm the address.

Now I am worried. *Does this place even exist?* I urgently wonder. *I found it on the internet,* I think with rapidly rising dread. *Was I scammed?* Meanwhile, my entire family is looking quizzically at the driver and then back at me. We are all a combination of excited to be here, fried from our long journey, and anxious to find our place. *Now what?* I think.

"Ah!" exclaims the driver. "Quindici via Verrazzano," pronouncing it "Ve-ra-*tza*-no" the proper Italian way, with the distinctive hard "tz" sound for the double z. "*Capisco!*"

"*Sì! Sì! Grazie!*" I reply, and we race off toward our new home.

Winding our way through Florence's narrow streets, we raptly absorb new sights and sounds. Motorbikes by the dozens loudly buzz through town, looking, sounding, and moving like swarms of bees. There is not a straight line more than a hundred feet, and we are turning every minute. *How does one navigate this city and not get lost?*

We finally pull into one of Florence's largest and most ancient public squares, Piazza Santa Croce. We circle three quarters around, hang a sharp right, and stop. Via Verrazzano is a short one-way side street formed with large, irregular cobblestones. It has narrow sidewalks on both sides that are not suitable for walking. They serve two purposes: for pedestrians to hop on in order to avoid oncoming cars, and for cars to park on to create a wider berth for moving vehicles, even if it makes pedestrian use impossible.

The street is lined on both sides by faded, mustard-colored, five-story-tall apartment buildings with narrow rectangular fronts. Most are connected to one another. Shutters hang off-kilter from many of the buildings' large windows, and small, decorative iron rails that serve no useful purpose are affixed to others. The buildings have street-level doors in muted colors. They might have been lustrous many years ago when they were last painted. There is no other architectural distinction in this scene; the street looks tired and old. Still, we are thrilled. It's our home away from home, and we're excited to finally be here.

Across the street stands a more modern apartment building. It is out of place in this old-world setting, but it does have a rare feature by Florentine standards: underground parking. It is a feature I will come to treasure. To call it a garage would be a stretch. It is small, dark, and narrow—*a perfect setting for the climactic scene in an Alfred Hitchcock film*, I will later think. At the end of the block is the street's one notable standalone structure, and it's magnificent. It is the oversized, villa-style ancestral home of the Verrazzano family. Giovanni da Verrazzano, who once lived here, was the first sixteenth-century European explorer to sail into what is now New York Bay.

Our realtor, Suzanne, is waiting for us in front of our building. Suzanne is late middle-aged, tall and thin, with blond hair and an angular frame. A true character, this assertive, wise-cracking Australian woman moved to Italy decades earlier and married an Italian man, and together they started a successful Florence-based real estate company. When I searched for apartments online, her company's website stood out for its quality. It primarily serves the extended-stay ex-patriot market, and it offers a host of services in addition to apartment rentals. She and her staff will prove to be invaluable travel concierges during our stay.

"Hello, you must be Art," Suzanne says, extending her hand to shake. "Welcome to Florence!" She warmly greets each of us. "Come on in!"

We step inside the lobby and immediately have to stop. It is still bright outside, but darkness quickly envelops us once we shut the heavy, dungeon-like door. We all take two steps up and process this scene as our eyes adjust to the dark. Directly in front of us is a tiny elevator. There is a wide, stone stairway up to its left. As the stairs steeply ascend, they wrap around the open elevator shaft.

"Who wants to take the first elevator ride up?" asks Suzanne, looking at our eager daughters. Kate and I look at each other with skeptical frowns. This tiny elevator can hold three or four people—maybe—but only if we squeeze tightly. Or it can hold a few suitcases. Or two little people and a couple suitcases.

Its size is one problem. My greater concern is that it looks terribly old, rusty, and dilapidated. Could it even reliably run? My dormant claustrophobia kicks in from out of nowhere. I immediately envision being trapped inside, my yells for help in this dark, dingy place going unheard for days. I feel the sweat forming on my warming brow.

"Um, Suzanne," I reply, coolly trying not to betray anxiety, "why don't we send our luggage up in the elevator, and we will all walk up the stairs."

"Are you out of your mind? That's four long flights up. Seventy-four steps! Didn't you just get off a transatlantic flight?" She looks at me, and then at Kate, incredulous.

Kate and I trade glances; we are on the same wavelength. "Yes, absolutely, we'll take the stairs," I reply. Jet lagged and exhausted, we all load the elevator with our gear, send it up, and trudge up the stairs. Our luggage is waiting for us at the top.

We enter our apartment and are met by a spacious, high-ceilinged living room with two large western-facing windows. The five of us stand there, taking it all in. The effect of the late-afternoon sunlight pouring in and filling the room with a warm, comfortable glow is especially striking after the dark-as-night hallway.

There is an old, out-of-tune baby grand piano at the near end. The rest of the room holds several pieces of mismatched furniture, chairs, a colorful rug that has seen better days, and a big red sofa with green throw pillows. At the far end, sitting on an old storage chest, is a small, old-fashioned black-and-white television with a rabbit-ears antenna on top. This eclectically furnished space looks every bit like the internet photos, and it feels like the perfect rental for a family with young children. I am pleased and relieved.

"Let's have a look around," Suzanne urges, disrupting our thoughts. She briskly begins a walkthrough. We amble past a tiny, functional kitchen space, through the dining room and its dated furnishings, and on to the bedrooms. The amply sized, sparsely furnished, nondescript master bedroom is up front. From there we enter a long hallway to access the rest of the apartment. That's when we notice the large, hermetically sealed window on the right facing a courtyard. It has a wide outside window sill with a flock of cooing pigeons, comfortably nesting amidst a small pile of desiccated feces.

Suzanne directs us into the oversized bathroom just off the hallway. It has the apartment's shower and bathtub, a toilet, and a tiny washing machine. After she shows us how to use the washing machine, I ask, "Is there a clothes dryer?"

Suzanne smiles knowingly. She walks Kate and me over to the bathroom window, opens it, and has us look outside. There are dozens of crisscrossing clotheslines serving four different buildings across a small courtyard. One is attached to a pulley within reach, just outside our window. "See this?" she says, as we survey this outdoor domestic scene. She then hands me a giant bag of clothes pins and drily says, "You get to have your own Italian clothes dryer." She breezily exits the bathroom, looks back, and says, "Let's see the other bedrooms, shall we?"

The girls' bedroom has two small beds with about a foot of space in between them and two small dressers. There is room for nothing else. The girls each immediately claim a bed and delightedly start jumping on them. We peek out their bedroom window and see the backs of three restaurants that open onto Piazza Santa Croce. Then it's on to the final room. Max's bedroom is not a bedroom. It is a small, pass-through den with a sleeping surface that is more couch than bed. Okay, a little false advertising for a value-priced apartment is not the end of the world. For a thirteen-year-old boy on an adventure, this will do. He seems satisfied.

Our day started thirty-six hours earlier in Minneapolis. It is now early evening in Florence. We are tired, but we are also hungry, hyper-stimulated, and ready to explore the new neighborhood. We excitedly head down the seventy-four steps to street level, where we are greeted by the warm Tuscan sun as it begins its slow descent over medieval Florence. Piazza Santa Croce is our nearby destination.

Santa Croce, at the piazza's head, is the largest Franciscan church in the world. It was completed in the early fifteenth century, after being under construction for two hundred years. Consistent with its Franciscan roots, this church, though magnificent on the inside, was built with a simple, homely exterior. The Florentine powers-that-be decided it was too plain for such a grand and historic structure, so in the mid-nineteenth century, they covered its front with a green-and-white neo-Gothic façade. This façade is now the visual that people associate with Santa Croce.

Santa Croce is best known for its many beautiful small chapels and their dozens of fresco paintings. Later in our stay, I will stand inside the church's Bardi Chapel with my other Florence art history classmates, listening to our instructor reverentially speak of its past. She will slow her delivery, and in a hushed tone dramatically raise her arm and point to one of the now-famous Giotto frescoes. She will then say, with a slow, dramatic flair, "And this . . .this very spot . . . is where the Renaissance began. It began with this painting." Creating an even greater impression on our children is that Santa Croce is the final resting place for many of Florence's most accomplished citizens, including Michelangelo, Galileo, and Machiavelli. Outside the church, facing the piazza, is a fifteen-foot-tall stone statue of Dante, majestically peering across the way.

The piazza itself is one of Florence's largest and most popular public spaces, though large is a relative term—I could slowly jog its circumference in less than two minutes. It is flanked by low-rise, centuries-old, fresco-covered buildings with faded, old-world charm. Their interiors hold pricey residential apartments. At street level there is a potpourri of restaurants, cafes, and touristy novelty shops. We will have no shortage of cheap, colorful choices for buying Max a souvenir soccer jersey before leaving Florence.

The piazza's center is all stone—no greenery at all, only a flat, paved surface. It has large, smooth, rectangular bricks that are ever-so-gently curved. They are brown with age. It is comfortable for walking, at least for short distances. Lining the piazza's edge are backless benches that are no more than a continuous row of smooth, stone slabs, mounted to a comfortable sitting height. There is a tall curb lining this space, requiring a big step up to reach the piazza's interior section.

The piazza is filled with people milling about, happily chatting away. There are parents, kids, elderly, a little bit of everything. Dogs tug at their leashes, also excited to partake in canine socializing. Some of the smaller kids ride bicycles, even though there isn't much open space. We will learn that by day, the piazza is a favorite tourist destination, but in the evening, the locals reclaim it. It's a lovely scene.

It's here that we first observe something we will always warmly associate with Italian life. It's characterized by the word *passeggiata*, which literally translated means leisurely stroll. But passeggiata is more than a word—it is a social activity and a lifestyle choice. Passeggiata is what families and couples do after a satisfying, shared dinner. They take a stroll down a popular street or through a public square or park where other neighbors are doing the same. People informally congregate and socialize. It is an integral part of *la dolce vita*, and it will become a favorite family activity.

We take a table at an outdoor trattoria, order pizza, and Kate and I gratefully have our first sips of the local Chianti Classico. We watch the square and absorb our noisy, colorful, home-away-from-home's surroundings. We are all lost in our thoughts, and this quiet contemplation lasts a minute or two. Max finally breaks the silence. "We're not leaving here, are we? I mean, why would anyone ever want to leave? This is amazing. I don't ever want to leave." Kate and I share soft smiles, tacitly agreeing. The *quattro formaggi* pizza and second glasses of wine make it even better.

14

La Dolce Vita

*I was in a sort of ecstasy, from the idea of being
in Florence [...] Absorbed in the contemplation of
sublime beauty [...] Everything spoke so vividly
to my soul [...] I had palpitations of the heart.*
—Stendhal

Once the kids' school starts, life develops a benign rhythm. My days begin with an early run, *The International Herald Tribune*, and a cup of coffee from La Luna Rossa, our neighborhood café.

My initial trip to the café provides a lasting lesson in Italian. On day one, the young barista and I develop a long-running game—she practices her English on me, and I counter with my early-stage Italian on her.

"*Latte, per favore.*"

"OK," she smilingly says, and she retreats to prepare my drink.

"Here it is," she says two minutes later, handing me my steaming drink.

"*Grazie.* Uh, *e bianco.* Is this *latte?*"

"*Si, latte.*"

I initially frown, and then lighten up. "*Ah . . . capisco!*" and I smile at my futility. "*Caffè latte, per favore,*" and I hand her back the cup of hot steamed milk.

My inner voice during morning runs is changed. It is still free-form and meditative, but on occasion, it's also more intentionally reflective on our new surroundings. I love absorbing novel sights and sounds while on foot, especially when traveling. I always have. My thoughts while running Florence inevitably migrate to a sense of wonder and gratitude. *How could my life have changed so much, so quickly, and so well? Is this real? How long can it last?* And occasionally my more practical, serious, and self-doubting inner voice creeps in, much as it dismays me. *How long do I even want it to last? When should I start thinking about being a responsible adult and going back to work? How long can I afford not to work?* I have no answers.

My thoughts inevitably return to the here and now. In my over-thinking way, I try forcing myself not to overthink. *Savor this moment for the gift it is,* I tell myself. I try to channel the wisdom of John Wooden, the greatest basketball coach of his generation and a personal leadership role model: "Make each day your masterpiece." It is fitting advice for a Florentine sojourn.

Getting the girls to and from school is a joy. Their school is a converted country villa. It is located several miles out of town in a setting that is gracefully nestled amongst Chianti's vineyards. I always volunteer for this driving task.

As we pass through the nearest town, Bagno a Ripoli, and then climb through the hills, I reconnect with a long-dormant source of pleasure—the love of driving. This is not the mind-numbing experience of driving Minnesota's flat, straight highways to and from work every day. It feels more like an amusement park simulation—up and down tortuous, hilly two-lane roads—with accelerations, braking, constant gear shifting, and breathtaking surprises around every corner. It is the kind of driving that causes squeals of laughter from the back seat. I get to do this every day. We are always rushing to get to school, but the solitary drives back are leisurely. I take different routes home, always less direct and more scenic.

I decided before leaving the United States that my first post-fifti-eth-birthday marathon would be in Italy. We arrive in Milan on a Saturday afternoon prior to Sunday's *Maratona di Milano* and imme-diately head over to the event's staging area. The finish line is in the shadow of the massive Milan Cathedral. This impressive neo-Gothic structure was begun in the fourteenth century and not completed until the early nineteenth century. What an amazing setting!

Marathon running is not yet in the Italian cultural mainstream, and staging an urban race is a logistical nightmare. Intersections are blocked, sort of, in order to allow runners through. This makes unknowing local drivers crazy. At each cross street there is a wild horn-honking fest. Drivers inch forward like an oncoming army, as they aggressively search for an opening in the wave of runners. Per-ceiving an opportunity, real or not, they gun their way through, even as the hapless *carabinieri* wave for them to stop. Runners frantically dodge the speeding cars. *This is crazy! Someone is going to get killed out here.* I have a couple near misses, and one time I miscalculate, stop short, and quickly reverse course.

There are other uniquely Italian characteristics that add to the event's charm. I find a block of Parmigiano-Reggiano cheese, a bottle of red wine, and a bag of gnocchi in my runner's goody bag. Along the course, there are masses of official volunteers who hand out bot-tled water and unpeeled bananas, resulting in countless wet banana peels and empty bottles after each water stop, as we all slip and slide along, trying to stay on our feet while waving our arms in cartoonish fashion to maintain balance.

I successfully complete the race with an assist from Max, who runs the final mile with me. One down and forty-nine to go! Two hours later, we check out of our hotel, and on our walk to the train station, we stop at a hole-in-the-wall trattoria for a post-marathon recovery meal. Scanning the menu, my eyes light up. Risotto alla Mil-anese. This aromatic, cheesy *primo piatto* has a rich, gooey texture, and saffron that delightfully bleeds orange streaks, begging to be gen-tly mixed. The taste is to die for. *Perfetto!*

What a gorgeous day! I can't believe that twenty-four hours ago I was in Milan running a marathon. It's a seasonably warm Monday morning in October. Even as my tired muscles throb with soreness, my brain explodes with endorphins. This post-marathon effect can last for hours or even a full day.

After dropping the girls off at school, I slowly pull out of the parking area, roll down my windows, and take a right toward my favorite route home. It's a narrow, twisty lane closely bordered on both sides by short stone walls. Various forms of climbing ivy and flowering plants intermittently cover the walls. It is a two-way road in theory, but it is wide enough for only one car. If another car approaches, which does not often happen, each driver looks for one of the small turn-offs to let the other go by.

Beyond both walls are groves of olive trees; narrow, pointy cypress trees reaching to the heavens; and grape vines, whose lines lazily undulate with the irregular Tuscan topography. More distant are farmhouses and small villas, framed inside a jigsaw puzzle of stone walls. The walls define property boundaries that are probably centuries old.

I turn on my car radio and flip channels. I have two favorites—one is the equivalent of popular tunes, and the other is opera. Today is a day for opera.

My God, this landscape is stunning, a thought no doubt elevated by my lingering runners' high. The operatic music is dramatic and perfect for this setting. I turn the volume way up. With all four windows wide open, it competes with the whooshing sound of air that is noisily and delightfully blowing through my moving car.

I slow down and roll to a stop, turn off the music, close my eyes, and pay no attention to whether or not cars approach from ahead or behind. I slump down in my seat, the sun's warming heat and a gentle breeze on my face. Taking a deep breath, I smell pine and flowering plants whose fragrance I cannot identify. Softly chirping birds are all that I hear. *Is there a more benign place on earth?* At complete peace, my eyes remain closed. *How did I get so lucky?*

Italy's rapturous, multisensory moments usually include an additional sense: taste. This trip reawakens my personal interest in food, not just eating it, but everything about it—food shopping, food preparation, meals of any kind, whether with family, friends, or even by myself, and even post-meal cleanup.

Long ago, in college, my friends and I talked about whether we eat to live or live to eat. For me, there is never any question. I have the good fortune to be in a country where it is embedded in the culture: Italians live to eat—meals are meant to be culinary and social events.

We are reminded of this national obsession at our first lower-school parent association meeting. The primary agenda item is not curriculum, teaching, safety, grading systems, or homework. No, nothing like that. What is foremost on everybody's mind, particularly for the Italian moms, is whether or not the cafeteria's pasta is prepared sufficiently *al dente*. This needs to be urgently addressed.

Kate and I relish this cultural food obsession and start many days with a trip to the local farmers' market to browse, shop, learn, and entertain ourselves. Along the way, we drop into the specialty food shops—the *pasticceria, forno, enoteca,* and of course the café. Sampling the fresh olive oils, cheeses, wines, or whatever we can find never gets old. Our favorite specialty food store is the hole-in-the-wall fresh pasta shop, with its long table, ancient and friendly pasta artisan, and jukebox-sized machine for theatrically rolling out and cutting pasta. We delight in leaving with a brown paper bag of freshly cut linguine and munching it along the way home.

A small group of ex-patriot parents organize to enrich our food-related experience. We hire a local woman to teach a weekly cooking class. Each class begins with a trip to the farmers' market to purchase ingredients. We plan meals with an emphasis on regional cuisine, preparing a sumptuous feast at each of our apartments on a rotating basis, and then eating. The wine also flows freely.

At our very first class, we receive an unexpected lesson. Preparing a carbonara sauce, we first fry up some bacon. After removing the bacon, the large cast-iron pan has a massive pool of bacon grease. Our instructor, Maria, tosses all of the other ingredients in and starts stirring. We all watch, look at each other, and make faces. Kate says what we are all thinking.

"Um, Maria, shouldn't we have drained all of that bacon grease? I mean, it's pure fat, and it's going to make us sick. Besides that, isn't it unhealthy?" We all nod in agreement. We aren't exactly food purists, but we also know that consuming large quantities of bacon grease is a bad idea.

Maria huffily turns around from the stove and stares Kate down. "I know how to cook! We know what we're doing in this country when it comes to food! Italians are *not* fat!" And she holds up her arms as if to say, "Look at me!" Maria, of course, has a stunning figure.

We all stare away, nobody saying a word. Our collective thought is, *Okay, she's the cooking expert, and we're guests in this country, so let's just go with it.* Of course, the carbonara turns out rich and delicious. In the end, we don't care about its nutritional value. We all gratefully lap up every drop and wash it down with local wine.

Max asserts his independence right away, and we are delighted. He insists on walking the two miles to school by himself every day. He leaves the apartment early, strolls through the awakening Piazza Santa Croce and its noisy truck sweepers, passes the massive nineteenth-century *biblioteca* (it is Italy's largest public library), crosses the Arno while peering downriver at the *Ponte Vecchio*, and climbs the long, winding, tree-lined avenue up to *Piazzale Michelangelo*, which displays the magnificent thirty-foot replica of Michelangelo's classic sculpture, *David*. Nearby he reaches the converted villa that is home to the International School's upper and middle schools. Prior to this move, because of our suburban location, he couldn't go anywhere without being driven. His world is fast-expanding.

Every now and then, if we get an early enough start, I accompany Max on his walk to school. I treasure these opportunities to connect while strolling through this magnificent, historical setting. He is always forthcoming in sharing details of his classes, his friendships, and his latest sporting activities. Among other things, he rediscovers his love for soccer while playing with his newfound friends from Europe and Latin America.

"So, Max, how does your day look?"

"It looks good! My history teacher has this fetish about Jack the Ripper. That was entertaining at first, but now it's getting a little old. Otherwise I'm liking school. The kids are great."

"Sounds good."

"How about you, Dad? How does your day look?"

"Let's see, what day is this?" I have to pause and think. "It's Tuesday."

"Tuesday? Yeah, it's Tuesday. Okay, so I have my cooking class all day."

He nods as he processes this. "Another stressful day at the office, huh Dad?"

Lower school pickup is an event, even on normal days. After school is social hour for both kids and parents. Kate and I always do this together. There's no way either one of us is going to miss out. There is a regular, comforting pattern to our pickups.

"Dad!" Elena delightedly cries. She runs into my arms as I stand in the courtyard, waiting with the other parents for school to let out.

"Hi dear, how was school today?" I say, returning the warm hug. "Where's Elizabeth?"

"She's not out yet," she says, as she looks back. "Oh, here she comes now."

"Hi, Elizabeth," and I spread my arms to greet her. She is tired and a little weepy by this time of day. Stamina is not this four-year-old's strength. She runs right past me to Kate, as she always does. Dad is a poor substitute for her mother's comforting hug.

"Lizzie, let's go to the maze," says Elena, as she runs through the door to the outer courtyard. Elizabeth recovers instantly and follows her sister.

The school's outer courtyard might be my all-time favorite setting. The entire space is comprised of a network of low bushes, forming a surprisingly complex maze. The walking paths are a dense pebble surface, and at major intersections stand three-foot-tall, weathered, earthen-colored terra-cotta vases. Kids love chasing each other through the maze, particularly right after school, delightedly solving spatial puzzles while at play.

Meanwhile, we parents sit on the stone benches chatting, distractedly watching the kids, and scanning the surrounding countryside. It is an unspectacular-yet-serene, thoroughly pleasing Tuscan landscape: a gently rolling hillside covered with dense, randomly growing olive trees; a modest vineyard; a separate area of well-spaced, orderly rows of olive trees; tiny patches of open grassland; and a long, horizontal row of cypress trees lining a distant hilltop like matchsticks. Even farther away, a couple of larger hills, always hazy, frame the foreground's more richly saturated hues, displaying a half-dozen shades of green. Because it is late afternoon, the sun shines directly on the hills. Its soft, golden light imparts a mood-enhancing glow. I am always inspired to pull out my camera and capture this perfect scene with a photograph. I take dozens of photos on several different occasions, and they always disappoint. I cannot capture digital perfection, no matter how many times I try or how many different ways I fiddle with the aperture and shutter speed controls.

Within a few minutes, the entire kid/parent group moves to the play area. It's a grove of olive trees and undersized conifers growing in loose, sandy dirt. They are framed by a background of low, rolling hills. Interspersed amongst the trees is playground equipment: a swing set here, a see-saw there, and a jungle gym behind the trees.

Social hour for parents continues through the kids' playtime. The parent group is about half Italian and half non-Italian, the latter mostly from other European countries and the United States. The ex-patriots all seem to be experiencing Italy according to the same formula as we are—taking a break from their conventional lives and trying to figure out where to go from here. Very few are formally employed while in Italy, although several have started small-scale entrepreneurial ventures. It is an accomplished, eclectic group and includes former and future diplomats, venture capitalists, an arms negotiator, an investment manager, journalists, and others from miscellaneous professional fields. We are connected by a love for our children, a growing connection to Italy, and an openness to family travel and adventure. Swapping travel stories is our favorite way to pass the time. A surprising number originally came to Florence intending to stay for only a year but decided to stay indefinitely.

"George flew for British Airways at the time," Robin, a British friend of ours, shares. "He flew us down in a small plane one spring, and we rented a flat outside Florence. Life sparkles here—it's so glorious to see the sun every day! We stayed on and on; we couldn't bring ourselves to leave. We kept buying new clothes. After three months, we looked at each other and said, 'Shall we go back to Britain to gather our things up?' He was finally able to catch on with BA here, and I found this school for Emma. So here we are!" She smiles a satisfied smile. Whenever Kate and I hear one of these stories, usually told in this glorious, pastoral setting, we share a knowing look and the same thought. *Hmm ...*

It is easy to pick out the Italian parents from the rest of us—they are the stylish ones. Always dressed to a T, the Italian moms wear pressed or silk blouses, fashionable slacks or skirts, shoes with heels, and flashy jewelry. Their hair and makeup are always just right, and they could easily go from the playground straight to an upscale restaurant for dinner.

It isn't just the women. The Italian dads wear crisp blazers over silk shirts, snazzy slacks, and fashionable, shiny shoes. And of course, every hair is always in place. The look is right out of a fashion magazine.

We ex-pats, meanwhile, lounge in our dowdy uniforms of blue jeans, tennis shoes, and faded polo shirts or other casual tops, feeling eclipsed, bemused, or oblivious. *I really need to upgrade how I dress. These guys look great,* I think with some envy. *I feel like such a schlump.* I make many mental notes to improve my casual wardrobe.

"Lizzie, we're home. Time to get up," I softly say, gently touching her head and then stroking her hair. It is late afternoon, and we just returned from school. I park in our dark little tunnel of a garage, and I hand the keys to Piero. He is our boyishly charming, chain-smoking, twenty-something parking attendant. He spends weekends hunting truffles with his specially trained dog, and he occasionally shares his treasures with us. He's a family favorite, and we always tip him well.

We gather our things and prepare for the walk up to street level, and then the seventy-four-step climb to our apartment. Lizzie's head tilts awkwardly as she breathes softly in her car seat, not stirring a whit. These long days tire her out completely, and the rides home are just the right tonic to induce sleep. I sigh, carefully reaching into the back seat and unbuckling her. *Here we go again.* I lean down and wrap my arms around her, extricating her without waking her or doing bodily harm to her or my own lower back from the awkward lifting motion. I carefully cradle her body, draw her out of the car seat, gently hoist her over my shoulder, and adjust my backpack. *Ready to go.*

The stair climbs normally don't bother me. We do them several times every day, and I tell myself that the extra exercise is a good thing. Besides, the only alternative is the creaky, old, never-inspected, closet-sized elevator with the emergency alarm that I'm sure doesn't work. It's the elevator that, if I took it, would get stuck. Nope, not for me—walking is fine. The only time the stair-climbing bothers me is after food shopping. I carry everything the three blocks home from the market, both by hand and on my back. It's tiring, but if I recruit a family member to help up the stairs, it works out fine.

Carrying a sleeping Elizabeth is another story. She is a forty-five-pound sack of potatoes, and there is nothing anyone can do to help. I enter our building's dark vestibule, stopping as I always do to let my eyes adjust from the bright outdoors to the poorly lit interior. I always take a few extra seconds when carrying her. I start the ascent, gingerly holding the railing with my free hand to steady myself, eyes continuing to adjust. The stone stairs are unforgiving, and there is no margin of error. As I pass the third floor on my way to the fourth, my brow warms and my heart pounds. Just eighteen more steps. We finally reach the fourth-floor landing. I slowly fish my keys out of my pocket, shifting Elizabeth ever-so-gently on my shoulder so that I can do this without waking her. I open the door on my second or third try, and we enter our apartment.

Once inside, and in one swift motion, Elizabeth stiffens her back and bolts up in my arms. Ear-to-ear devilish grin, she cries, "Fooled you again, Dad! I wasn't sleeping!"

The choice for our evening activity is always up for grabs.

"Let's go out and get some gelato for dessert," I suggest.

"You always want to go out for gelato, Dad," a smiling Elena observes.

"Yeah, I guess I do," I sheepishly reply.

"I've got homework, Dad. Count me out," says Max.

"I'll pass tonight, too, Art. I'd like to do some reading," Kate chimes in. She's in marathon training mode, and by this time of day, she is ready for a well-earned break.

"Okay, girls, it's just the three of us. We can skip the gelato. How about we go to the Piazza?"

"Yeah, let's go to the Piazza." They light up, and we head for the door.

The Piazza is our passeggiata, except we do it with our own distinctive style. I race the girls down the stairs, and we burst out the door. "Let's run!" And the race continues the half block to the Piazza.

This large, concrete public square, a bit severe but still a lovely evening scene, is our playground. It is always Family Night Out after dinner in our neighborhood, and that means three generations of family members casually socializing. The restaurants do a lively al fresco business. Music gently wafts through the square, coming from the open-air restaurants and an occasional strolling musician. There is a faint aroma of garlic-infused red sauce, and the shops are reopened for the evening. It is a relaxing, Italian-style urban evening vibe, a cool, low-level hum, and we love it.

"Dad's It!" says Elena. "Dante is the safe base," referring to the massive statue at the Piazza's far end. The girls take off. They have no inhibitions as they gleefully weave their way through the crowds toward Dante. I always give them a couple seconds' head start, and then I lazily jog in their direction.

Within a half hour, we are walking back to our apartment.

"I'll give you a one floor head start, girls, and tonight I'm going to win."

The upstairs sprint is on, laughter loudly reverberating through the capacious, ancient stone stairwell. They always just barely win, of course. Bedtime comes quickly, and they settle in for the night.

Traveling with our children turns out to be much easier than expected. We are fortunate to have three resilient, adventurous kids. Beyond that, it is often an entertainment pleasure. That is not to say we don't have our moments. Just two weeks into our Italy experience, Elizabeth famously melted down when she heard the word *duomo* in our family conversation. *Duomo* is a generic reference to domed churches. Florence has a large and beautiful one, and it is simply referred to as The Duomo. Many Italian cities we visit have duomos, and we have already toured several. We enjoyed visiting them—or so I thought.

"Duomo! Duomo! I hate duomos!" four-year-old Elizabeth cried out, interrupting our conversation and startling all of us. "I never want to see another duomo. Never! Ever!" She burst into tears, sobbing uncontrollably for several minutes at the thought of this vile word. As we consoled her, I silently smiled. I was pretty tired of touring duomos too.

Our kids generally engage well in our touring activities, although you never really know what will capture their imaginations. We have a week's break at mid-semester, and we go to Istanbul, Turkey. At Topkapi Palace, we learn about the Ottoman Empire, the palace's history, and some of its famous inhabitants. Not surprisingly, the girls want to learn more about sultans and Turkish princesses. They are squarely in their Disney princess phase. Max, as one might expect from a teenage boy, is fascinated by the guide's description of the harems and wants to learn more about what goes on there. After the guide tells him they were managed by eunuchs, Max turns to me.

"Dad, what's a eunuch?"

"What?"

"What's a eunuch?"

I think for a moment, not quite sure how to explain this to my teenage son. "It's a man who's been castrated." Seeing his quizzical look, I elaborate. "You know, a guy who's had his testicles cut off."

"Huh?" His eyes widen, his brow furrows, he looks down for a couple seconds and slightly shakes his head before saying, "That's got to be like the worst job in the world."

The whole Italy plan came together quickly the prior summer. We had our tickets and updated passports, the kids were enrolled in school, we had an apartment, and we were taking off for Florence three weeks after hatching the plan. Yes!

Then it dawns on me. *I wonder if there any other requirements for entering the country?* I google "Italian visa," and my heart sinks. There it is—if you stay for more than ninety days, you need a *permesso di soggiorno* (permission to stay).

Thank God—there's an Italian consulate in St. Paul. They'll help me.

"*Buongiorno*, you have reached the Italian consulate in St. Paul, and I am Francesca. We are here to answer all of your questions about our lovely country. We are currently on vacation for the month of August and will return on September 1st. Please leave a message. Ciao."

Not that I have to, but I look at our flight departure tickets anyway. August 31. *Oy, now what?*

"Buongiorno, Mr. Arthur, I am Giorgio, and you have reached the Chicago office of the Italian consulate. How may I help you today?"

As I explain the situation, he interrupts, "Si, capisco. You can come to our office and apply in person. It is the only way. The lines are very long, and we may not be able to see you for a day or two."

"What?" *Forget it! We'll take our chances.*

A few months later, sitting in our Florence apartment, I think about this again. *We can stay as long as we want. We'll just continue to stay under the radar,* I smugly reassure myself. *How could they possibly find out that we're not properly documented?*

The next day, on my way to pick up the girls at school, I distractedly look at the clock. Chronically late, I accelerate around the corner. I immediately hear a police siren.

Uh oh, I quietly think, my heart skipping a beat as my mind races through the consequences of being deported.

"Ciao, Signore Poliziotto," I stammer.

He jabbers something rapidly in Italian. I don't understand his words, though I know what he is asking.

I respond, "*Che cosa? Non capisco. Non parlo l'Italiano.*"

I point to myself and sheepishly smile, "Americano." I shrug my shoulders and try very hard, without needing to, to be the clueless American tourist.

"Ah . . . Americano!" He smiles. That explains everything. He rolls his eyes, walks back to his car, and drives away.

"Art, Mom is not well," Kate says, as she settles into the car and stares straight ahead, her face a wall of worry. "I don't know what to do about her."

I ease away from the airport's arrivals area, gently merging into Florence's constantly flowing traffic. She is returning from several days in Detroit, where she caught up with her mother.

"What's going on?" I ask.

"She's so forgetful and unfocused. She's got cognitive issues. She's just not herself." She pauses several seconds and then continues, "I think she has Alzheimer's. No, I'm sure she has Alzheimer's."

"What? Alzheimer's? Really?" I am incredulous. "How can that be? She's still driving, right? And running? And playing tennis? She's socially active too. Isn't she just sixty-nine years old?"

"Yes, I know," she dully replies, continuing to stare straight ahead, lost in her thoughts.

We both understand this situation's gravity. We are all too familiar with Alzheimer's. I lost Dad to it earlier in the year, following many years of steady decline. It's a horrific disease, and it puts a terrible strain on caregiving families.

Kate perks up and assertively continues. "I'm telling you, there's a major problem here. I'm sure of it. She gets confused easily, and now she's forgetful. She got lost on a bike ride in our neighborhood. She's losing her mind." Worry in her voice, she calmly concludes, "Art, she's very vulnerable. This is a disaster in the making."

"So, what are you thinking?" I knew that she already thought this through, planning out all the possibilities and contingencies. Kate is a planner.

"She's being tested at the University of Michigan. But that doesn't matter, it's not going to tell me anything I don't already know. I have to think about going home. This is only going to get worse. We don't have a lot of options here, and I'm the only one who can give her the care that she needs." Being an only child and having no other close family members, Kate knows what is coming—she is going to be her mom's primary caregiver.

We wait for an opportune time, a few days later, to discuss it further. By then we both had time to process these new facts. We agree that there is only one viable choice—at the end of the fall semester, we are going home. This disease is a terrible and ultimately tragic development for my mother-in-law. She needs us, and we need to help her. Our open-ended sojourn in Italy will end less than five months after it began.

We are sad to give up our carefree, stimulating life abroad. A family chapter is truncated prematurely. La dolce vita is glorious and all too short. We arrived in Florence with high hopes and prepared to have an open-ended adventure. Now, just before Christmas of 2006, we book our trip back to Minneapolis to resume our pre-Italy lives.

I surprise myself, realizing that part of me is looking forward to returning home. I feel ready to engage in a new professional phase, to get back at it. To get back at what? I'm not sure, but my practical voice is always present. *Italy's been great, but it's time to be responsible and get back to work.*

The flight attendants briskly walk up the aisle, snapping the overhead bins shut as they go. We hear a long message in Italian, and then the familiar English translation. "Tray tables should be placed in their upright and locked positions. All large electronic devices should be turned off and stowed during takeoff . . ." There's lots of white noise as the little fans above every seat loudly blow air through the cabin.

Here we go! I scan across our row. Kate is already into her book, *Brunelleschi's Dome*, a story of how Florence's Santa Maria del Fiori's (The Duomo's) dome was designed and built in the fifteenth century. She and I share a practice of reading books that are set in the places we visit. I am working on the Michelangelo biographical novel *The Agony and the Ecstasy*. The kids are already happily scanning the flight's video offerings. Travel time is a treat for them, as in our normal day-to-day, we do not allow them screen time. Observing them, then peacefully settling in, I put my book down, turn, and stare straight ahead. My thoughts wander back to my prior life. It hasn't been that long, but it feels like a life that I now struggle to recognize. I certainly don't miss it.

I frequently flew overseas in my earlier working life, always in premium class. Not one to sit still, even on an airplane, I often walked up and down the plane's length. I felt bad for the people traveling in coach class on long international flights, stuck sitting nearly upright in cramped-looking seats. There were typically a lot of young people, older people, and families. Having young children myself, I particularly noticed parents traveling with small children. That looked like pure misery, and I often thought about how fortunate I was to be traveling in solitude, comfort, and peace at the front of the plane.

Years later, beginning with this trip, I experience overseas flights completely differently. Our family camps out in coach class, and our kids are well prepared with their books, videos, games, and other "busy bag" distractions.

A couple hours into our flight, I revert to my old practice—I get up and stroll. Approaching the premium-class section, I observe that most people are traveling alone. Knowing that I used to be one of them, now I feel bad for them. *These people are traveling great distanc-*

es by themselves. I am lucky—I get to spend this time with my family. I do not miss the creature comforts or calm solitude of business-class travel, now preferring the closeness and barely controlled chaos of coach-class family travel.

I return to my seat. Kate is still reading, and the children are absorbed in their videos. Staring out the window, I'm mesmerized by the dark, shimmering, gently rippling ocean miles below. It's crowned by a cloudless sky that stretches to infinity into rich, graduated shades of blue.

15

WHAT'S NEXT?

I saw the angel in the marble and
carved until I set him free.

—Michelangelo

This question unnerved me when I contemplated leaving Ameriprise—*what's next?* I had no answer, and it was paralyzing. I still have no answer, but now anxiety is replaced by optimistic energy. La dolce vita allowed me to reorient, reboot, refresh, and renew. At the time, I didn't fully understand why, but I desperately needed that. It nurtured hope, if not clarity. *I'll figure it out and be open to anything,* or so I thought.

Immediately upon returning home, though, and without conscious intent, I retreat to my comfort zone, as old thought and behavior patterns reemerge. It's as if I never left, and within weeks, I begin a conventional job search. I dive right in and am pleased to find there are interesting leadership opportunities available.

I am in a nondescript, suburban office park, checking my interview appointment notice against the building numbers to find the right one. The dozen or so buildings all look the same—low-rise, connected, generic, boxy structures. These offices are conveniently located on a service road just off of the interstate, about a dozen miles from downtown. A physical work setting could not be less inspiring. The chilly, gray February day reinforces its bleakness. *I suppose the rent is low*, I muse, thinking that's probably a good thing. I am not excited as I open my car door and bundle up against the cold. *Okay, let's do this.*

"Good morning, Art," greets Peter, the smiling CEO of an early-growth-stage financial services firm. An industry veteran with the white hair and warm, reassuring manner to match, he launched his firm with "funding from friends and family." It's on the cusp of taking off. "We'll be ready to go public in less than two years. I'm looking for a finance and strategy partner."

Got it. I know this drill. "I have the experience you're looking for, Peter," I confidently say as I launch into my pitch. "I spent the last decade working with Wall Street bankers, developing capitalization strategies, and doing large financings." *Blah blah blah.* I am on auto-pilot, reaching back and finding a mental muscle I haven't exercised in a long time. It feels both natural and strange. It's me talking, but it feels like an out-of-body experience, and I am a bemused, cynical observer.

Peter listens attentively. His body language alternates between inscrutable and modestly positive. He smiles at the right times and maintains steady eye contact. He asks a few more questions and then shifts to a selling mode. "I think you're well-suited for this, Art, and you'll be the partner I need. Are you interested?" he asks directly.

Why am I unprepared for this question? "Absolutely!" I reply with a smile, doing my best to fake it. *Shoot, I don't know.*

This is perfect on paper. But my gut is saying no.

I would have jumped on this a year ago. But not now. *What happened? How have I changed? If I turn my back on this, then what?*

This is remarkably similar to a feeling I had in another recent interview. I rationalized that one: bad chemistry, uncomfortable fit, something is off. Whatever it is, I trust my gut. This time, it's the same scenario: a good opportunity, and it's there for the taking. But I'm not feeling it.

Hold it! I have three kids and a mortgage. I need to work. What in the world am I going to do?

Peter is not picking up on my ambivalence as we warmly shake hands and agree to meet again in a week. Good. I'll keep my options open, just in case I change my mind in the next few days. *What am I saying? That's not going to happen.*

Arthur C. Brooks, the former president of the American Enterprise Institute, did an Aspen Ideas Festival presentation in 2018 on how professional decline is inevitable with age, how to gracefully deal with that, and even how to turn it to your advantage for a happier second half of life. He wrote a similarly themed article for *The Atlantic* in July 2019 titled "Your Professional Decline Is Coming (Much) Sooner Than You Think."

Brooks drew on Hindu teachings to describe two life stages that provide context. There's a period during our early adulthood and middle age, called *Grihastha*, where we focus on building successful careers during an extended growth phase. Professionally speaking, one's "foot is on the gas" as we focus on more "earthly rewards" such as money and power. He contrasts this to the stage that follows, starting roughly at the age of fifty, called *Vanaprastha*. In this subsequent stage, we slowly ease our foot off the gas and shift to be more service-oriented, spiritual, and relationship-focused. As we do, we "resist the conventional lures of success in order to focus on more transcendentally important things."

Brooks suggests that two different artistic processes, painting and sculpting, metaphorically describe these two life stages. We each start life with the equivalent of a blank canvas. During our early adulthood and middle-aged period—the *Grihastha* phase—we add the greatest level of detail and complexity to our lives: we complete our formal educations, get jobs, build relationships, construct careers, create families, and acquire wealth. This process is comparable to a painter continuously adding brushstrokes to a canvas over many years, creating a complex piece of visual art. The metaphorical result is a painting that accumulates richness and depth, representing how one's life uniquely grows and develops during this phase.

In contrast to painters, who create by adding, sculptors create by chipping away. This style of creative art represents the *Vanaprastha* phase that begins in later mid-life. Sculptors start with a simple, massive block of stone such as marble. To a sculptor, the art already exists deep inside the stone, but it needs an artist's vision and skill to be discovered. This happens through a process of exploring, experimenting, and continuous shaping and reshaping. The sculpting process is addition by subtraction, and refining what emerges.

In this life phase, as we "purposefully focus less on professional ambition, and become more and more devoted to spirituality, service, and wisdom," we remove, reshape, and simplify in order to expose more fundamental truths. We reveal ourselves in the process, and in ways that were previously unknown, or just vaguely known and underdeveloped. We focus on more essential qualities such as creating deeper, more meaningful relationships; engaging in the world in different ways, often by giving back to our communities; pursuing personal interests, perhaps rediscovering interests and underdeveloped talents from earlier in our lives; and continuously exploring new learning opportunities. It's a time to gain deeper insights, to form stronger connections, to live more intentionally, and to be guided by a greater sense of social purpose.

I heard Brooks's presentation more than a decade after returning from Italy. The light immediately went on. When I had the job interview with Peter, I didn't understand the "what" or the "why," but in the moment, I sensed that my mid-life pivot was happening. Lacking the vocabulary, I could not explain why I reacted negatively. Now I know—I was seeking purpose, something more personally meaningful. But at the time when I asked *what's next,* I had no answers, only confusion and a gut feeling that I had to keep looking.

I'm perplexed by my reaction to these job interviews. Seeking clarity, I take a variety of assessments. I actively network while also receiving guidance from professional career counselors and friends. These approaches all point me toward more people-centered, relationship-based paths. I built my career staring at a computer, analyzing financial data, and solving quantifiable problems. Now my instincts are leading me in a completely different direction. This is revelatory. Teaching rises to the top of my list. This makes sense to me. After all, Mom and Dad were teachers. *Maybe it's in my DNA*, I think. In recent years, I also enjoyed engaging with young professionals in mentoring and coaching roles, so I explore higher-education opportunities. It's my first experiment as I start chipping away on a path to discovery. I become an adjunct finance instructor at a couple local universities.

At one school, I have the additional role of "Executive Fellow." Among other things, I do leadership presentations for new MBA students. My favorite message is to be courageous, get out of your comfort zone, and take risks. It is the surest path to personal and professional growth. I share a story I heard a decade earlier at a business conference.

"There is a winter Olympics event called the luge. A luge is a tiny sled. You lay down on your back, with feet on the downhill side. You then descend an icy, narrow, steep, twisting tubular track at high speed until you reach the course's bottom. The objective is to finish in the fastest possible time. By all accounts, it is thrilling and extremely dangerous. Our story's protagonist has a lofty goal: he wants to try the luge and dreams of making the national team. There is one problem: he is too afraid to try it. He thinks about it for years. It is something completely outside his experience, and the thought of it fascinates and scares him.

"Finally, he gets up the courage, travels to the Lake Placid, New York luge course, and creates an opportunity to take his first run on it. As he ascends the stairs to the top, he is terrified, and he begins to have second thoughts. He considers turning around. He slows his pace as he continues ascending. Standing at the top and looking down, his heart is exploding in his chest. He wavers: 'Do I have the courage to do this?'

"He stands at the precipice and looks down for a minute. Finally, he drops off the edge and onto the track with his sled, and screams,

"Oh shit!" He begins a steep plunge to the bottom. This is his "Oh Shit Moment," or OSM. OSMs happen the very moment you pass a point of no return while taking a risky, decisive action. Our friend took a huge risk. There was no taking it back, and he just had a monumental OSM. The good news is that he gets to the bottom and is giddy with delight. He has newly found confidence and courage. He knows he can do this, and he does it over and over again. Eventually he becomes a national-class competitor."

My students and I discuss how this "feel the fear and do it anyway" story gives us permission to feel fear and anxiety, knowing that failure is possible. This feeling is necessary in order to stretch, learn, and grow. The story's point is that we all need to seek out more OSMs. It's the only way to grow, and that search should never end.

Living with intention and courage is something I want to do. Telling this story to students is a much-needed personal reminder. *What more can I do to get out of my comfort zone?*

I am enjoying teaching, though I also explore another path: leading a nonprofit. I am drawn to community service, harkening back to my parents' strong community orientation and my own early career choices.

The greatest positive influence on me, though, is Kate. She's encouraging, but it's not her words that move me. It's the choices she has consistently made over many years, choices that I have always quietly admired. She volunteers in both big and small ways—community board member, engaged parent volunteer, after-school tutor, fundraiser. Her jumping in to fill a community leadership void after 9/11 was quintessentially Kate. Shortly after that, when we shared with friends that we were moving from New Jersey to Minnesota, one looked at her in disbelief and literally sputtered, "But . . . but . . . you can't leave us! You're a *pillar* in the community!"

While Kate and I share these core community values, she is the one who consistently acts; I am the one who observes, encourages, and applauds, but stays on the sidelines. While cheering her on, I rationalized, *I'm too busy to engage right now.* "Right now" has extended for two decades. Her activist spirit and philanthropic heart are a guiding light for my new phase.

The large, troublesome disparities in our community—in education, healthcare, housing, employment—are everywhere. My more idealistic self, long dormant, is ready to contribute. I take a couple community board positions as a means to engage and learn. As I do, the idea of applying my corporate leadership experience to run a nonprofit service program intrigues me. I extend my network, seeking out people who can help me to learn more.

That's when I meet John. I see him as a potential role model for what I want to do, and I am excited to learn from his experience. We have not previously met. A mutual friend made this connection on my behalf.

It's early morning, and the nondescript Minneapolis skyway coffee shop is still quiet.

"Hi John, thanks for your time today."

"Sure, Art," John smiles in return. "It's always fun to share my experiences with a fellow corporate fugitive."

John is a forty-something former senior corporate executive who now runs a large healthcare nonprofit. He is high energy, smart, and opinionated. He is a big guy—tall and broad-shouldered—and looks like he might have played hockey in his younger days. With his large frame, curly brown hair, wire-rim glasses, and confident style, it's not a stretch to picture him in a corporate executive suite.

John's career switch is a model for what I'm considering. His leadership reputation is strong. The corporate leaders I know who switched to run nonprofits are generally successful, some famously so. *Leadership skills are universal, I think, and large companies provide great training for later-in-life sector transitions.* At least that's my theory. I expect John to sell me on the value of taking a service leadership role.

"Well," he coyly begins, smiling and leaning back in a reflective pose, "it's not everything it's cracked up to be." He loses his smile as he continues, getting right to the point. "Yeah, I do get a lot of satisfaction from helping people. We do great work in this community. Yeah, that feels good. But you know what really sucks? It's the fundraising part. Day-to-day, I interact very little with the people we serve."

He makes direct eye contact and leans forward, and I feel the intensity of his gaze as he continues. "My job is to ask people for money. That's what I do every day. I ask people for money. It's not a lot of fun." He pauses as he contemplates a question, relaxing a little. "So, are you looking to take a finance role or to be a CEO?"

"I'd only go in as a CEO," I reply. I've not held a CEO job, but I am ready to step up and lead an organization. I believe that. Besides, after a long corporate career and at my age, I have no interest in having another boss.

"Are you a salesman?" he asks.

I smile and say, "No, anything but . . ."

"Then stay away from this sector," he sharply interjects. "Don't do it. It'll make you miserable."

He sees my questioning look. "Do you want to fundraise for a living?" he asks, again leaning in, eyebrows raised, as if to underscore his point. The meeting ends quickly.

I started this conversation with optimism, expecting to hear an inspirational story of service-oriented leadership. I walk out in a fog, slowly trudging through the now-bustling morning skyway, oblivious to the fast-moving foot traffic that flows around me. John just threw up on my plan. *No, I don't want to make a living out of asking people for money. I would be terrible at that, and I'd hate it. Now what?*

Unable to find a singular satisfying career path, I settle into a professional portfolio of varied activities: I am a part-time teacher, a part-time treasurer for a small public company, a business advisor to a financial education company, and a volunteer board member. This wasn't my plan, but it works fine as I continue to ask myself, what *is* the plan? I'm in no hurry, and maybe this is it. I feel engaged, and I also have time for the rest of my life.

Family is my top priority, and it is more important than ever. In addition to spending time with Kate and our three children, my mother-in-law now lives with us. Her Alzheimer's diagnosis was confirmed, and we moved her from her Michigan home into our house. Kate is her primary caregiver. I become her part-time concierge, cook, and chauffeur—driving her to appointments and generally trying to give Kate relief when I can. Caregiving for an Alzheimer's-afflicted elder is exhausting. Kate bears most of that burden, and the emotional toll is heavy. Our children and I help however we can.

I also have the time to develop personal interests. Running marathons becomes a major focus, amongst my many activities. The daily training is a grind, but I enjoy the benefits. I enthusiastically pursue my goal of completing fifty marathons after turning fifty years old.

I take piano lessons for the first time in decades. It sticks, and I rediscover a long-dormant love for music's calming, restorative, and soul-enriching impact. I enter an extended Gershwin period with high hopes. I feel accomplished when I can eventually perform two Gershwin Preludes and an improvisational version of "I've Got Rhythm" at student recitals.

I continue to nurture my love for cooking—a love enhanced by Italy—and I appreciate our family meal times more than ever. On a whim, I purchase one of Lynne Rossetto Kasper's *The Splendid Table* series of cookbooks. I then work my way through most of it, much to my family's delight. Then I buy another, and another.

I proactively chip away the layers to reveal my new life. I experiment, discover, and rediscover, and many parts of it are just as I had hoped. I am doing this deliberately, but on occasion, there are delightfully random opportunities as well.

"Congratulations to Adam and his teammates for winning the gold medal at the Senior Games." I see Adam's picture on Facebook, posted by his wife, Alison, and I am curious and a little envious. Adam and I were basketball teammates in college. It's been twenty-five years since I last saw him and Alison. Fittingly, that day twenty-five years earlier, Adam and I played a brutal series of one-on-one basketball games near his Connecticut home. A mutual love for the game and shared on-court experiences make reconnecting feel very easy.

"Tell Adam congratulations!" I comment on Alison's post. "Tell him if he ever needs an extra player for a basketball tournament to let me know." Within an hour I hear from Adam, and we have our first conversation in twenty-five years.

"Art, are you serious about playing? Because we have a tournament in two weeks in Portland, Maine, and we could use you. Can you make it?"

"Yes! I'd love to play. Thanks, Adam!" Even in my fifties, and not having touched a basketball in many years, I answer without hesitation. As a basketball junkie, although now only in spirit, I'm thrilled for the opportunity to play ball again.

"Great," he replies. Then, hesitatingly, he asks, "By the way, can you still play?" I understand the question. Once-athletic bodies and skill sets are typically distant memories by late middle-age. And I know Adam. Even at this stage of life, he's a fierce competitor, always playing to win.

"Yes!" I immediately respond.

I honestly don't know, but it'll be fun to try.

By my modest definition of success—avoiding injury and embarrassment—I succeed. And though I contribute little, the team wins the tournament. With time, I am able to scrape a little rust off of my game, and I'm invited back for more tournaments. I am a role player on a very good team, and we go on to be regular qualifiers at the National Senior Games' Three-on-Three basketball competition. Even better, I connect with a great group of Boston-based guys, unified by a love for the game.

There are also false starts. Years earlier, inspired by Dad, I became an occasional golfer. Dad got pleasure from the game to the very end. Even when he was ninety years old and completely lost in an Alzheimer's haze, I took him to a driving range. He was barely ambulatory, understood little, and was unable to speak coherently. I hit some balls as he watched. Holding up my club toward him, I then asked if he wanted to hit a few, not really knowing if this was a good idea. He smiled and nodded. I helped him over to the tee box, set up a ball for him, handed him a club, and stepped back. *This will be interesting*, I thought, though I had more worry than curiosity. He hadn't held a golf club in years, and I had no idea what to expect, or even if he could stand on his own for ten to fifteen seconds. He stepped right up, addressed the ball, started his familiar silky-smooth backswing, bent his back leg ever so slightly, twisted his hips in perfect form, and "ker-pow!" (as he would have said in his younger days). It was the Bob Berman of old. He still had game.

Reflecting on this and the lifetime of pleasure he derived from golf, I decide that now's the perfect time for me to get into it, to finally develop my game. I venture out to the driving range, thinking how happy this would make Dad. Eying my large bucket of balls, I grab a five-iron and warm up. I smugly think, *The journey back begins.*

I had at best been a pretty bad golfer, but this day, I plumb new depths of futility. I occasionally even whiff completely. *Is it possible to suck more at something?* With each swing-and-miss, I sheepishly look around, amused and horrified, and wonder if anyone else saw what just happened. *My God, this is embarrassing.* Then I hit bottom with my next swing. I create a long divot that starts more than a foot behind where the ball still sits. I snap a photo, memorializing my failed experiment. Leaving dozens of unhit balls behind, I walk away from the game forever. *Sorry, Dad.*

16

FIFTY AFTER FIFTY

I'll be happy if running and
I grow old together.
—Haruki Murakami

There's always a next marathon on my schedule. It's a welcome added incentive to train, and training is my daily drug. Regular runs calm my nerves, lift my mood, fortify my resilience, and keep me physically fit. I run two or three marathons a year, and thankfully my body is responding well. I gain speed through my fifties, running my fastest race in more than twenty years at the age of fifty-six. This surprises and delights me. Better yet, I enjoy it, another pleasant surprise, particularly in light of a couple of inauspicious early running fiascos.

The whimsical goal I set when leaving Ameriprise—running fifty marathons after the age of fifty—is artificial, and it may be unrealistic. It was meant to keep me focused, and it serves that purpose. I got off to a good start in Italy one month after turning fifty. As of this writing (I am now in my mid-sixties), I'm still on track, and if all goes well, I will achieve my goal in my early seventies. If I can achieve it, great; if I can't, *c'est la vie.* I'm giving it my best shot.

I'll keep going until I am physically unable, or until I simply decide that enough is enough. That could happen in two months, two years, or two decades. There are relatively few people my age who run marathons, and I am learning that there are good reasons for that. Marathon training takes a toll on joints and muscles, and aging bodies are more injury-prone, less resilient, and less energetic. Thankful for the gift of good health, and knowing that my luck could turn at any time, I don't make plans beyond my next race.

It's difficult for some to understand why anyone in his right mind would regularly run marathons. It's also hard to explain. Non-runner friends and acquaintances typically respond with a combination of two reactions: admiration and an unspoken *"are you nuts?"* attitude. Perfectly rational people correctly point out the many less risky, less demanding ways for someone to stay physically fit. Some, perhaps more than I realize, think I'm obsessive for running marathons at my age. They are probably right. One has to have a bit of an obsessive/compulsive issue to train as I do. Within the endurance sports world, though, I have seen much worse, and my approach is not an obsession. I tell myself that it's a good thing, an uncompromising commitment to health and well-being. *It's more about lifestyle than sport*, I think, and that becomes even more true with time.

Races are brutally intense. To some extent, that's a choice, as part of the reason is my attitude. I set challenging goals for each race and push hard to the end. If I'm not hyperventilating the last few miles, then I'm not trying hard enough. When done, it feels like I've been hit by a truck. Waking up the next morning, despite my aches and pains, I feel elated, accomplished, and empowered. Even as my physical abilities are diminishing, with each completed marathon, it feels like I am achieving far more than I ever dreamed.

There are many other positives to maintaining a high level of aerobic fitness: improved emotional resilience; better sleep; shared experiences and friendships with other runners; the freedom to indulge in favorite foods; and travel to destination events, participating in such exhilarating experiences as the Boston and New York City Marathons. Kate and I have run them together, an added benefit, and these shared experiences make them even better. Perhaps the best unintended consequence is that we can be positive role models for our children—setting ambitious personal goals, committing to a plan, working hard, and never making excuses. We have a family tradition that the children run with us the final mile to the finish line, making each experience even better.

Advancing age is becoming an issue, and I am both quietly resistant and accepting of the inevitable. I still have high energy and endurance, but I am also slowing down. A lot. The emotional part of getting through each event is easier with age. For years I had high anxiety before a race, knowing what was coming. Now I have none. Now I feel only gratitude, knowing how lucky I am to be out there competing. The physical part of racing is still hard. I accept that I will suffer—all runners do. That's just an inseparable part of the experience.

Marathoners all fail from time to time. I had an epic failure in one Boston Marathon in particular, when I dropped out at mile twenty-five, suffering from severe hypothermia. I'd reached a point where I couldn't move a muscle, and I had the irrational thought that I might die if I continued. As numbness overtook my entire body, I barely shuffled to a nearby medical tent and made an on-the-spot decision that I was done. Living another day was worth the disappointment of my only DNF (did not finish).

Knowing failure is always possible, even when well prepared, keeps marathoners humble. We give it our all, and now that faster times are no longer achievable, commitment to training, competing, best effort, and just staying healthy enough to power through the next race are themselves the goals. I used to quietly scoff at "participation" medals that kids get for showing up to play. Now, for me, participation means success, because I've stayed healthy enough to keep at it. Finisher medals have become cherished souvenirs.

Running marathons is worth the physical stress and risks. Aside from its many other benefits, marathoners experience peak moments in time that remain indelibly etched in memory. Sometimes it's a visual. Sometimes it's a feeling. Sometimes it's an experience with other runners, like a pre- or post-marathon meal. It could be anything, and it could happen at any time. They are often spontaneous, and they can trigger an emotional response.

Sometimes my peak moments come before a race even starts. These are times where my nervous excitement, at least in my younger days, is barely contained. After preparing for months, at that very moment before starting, I have an explosive amount of pent-up energy. The "Star-Spangled Banner" is often played. When I attend other sporting events, I usually mouth the words but do not sing. But before marathons, I enthusiastically belt out the words.

At New York City, the race starts with the shooting of a cannon. Then Frank Sinatra's "New York, New York" is blasted over the public-address system, as the runners whoop it up, sing and dance, and festively cross the start line. We head onto the Verrazzano-Narrows Bridge for a stunning view of the harbor and city. At the Pike's Peak Marathon, we sing "America the Beautiful" at the start, staring off at a distant Pike's Peak that we will soon climb. Cast against a sunrise of pink and purple, it is the very location that inspired the song's words "purple mountains' majesty." In Milan, shortly after a Sunday morning start, we run down a splendid wide avenue of classic European elegance, breathe in the mouth-watering smells of freshly baked pastries and brewed coffee, and hear a thunderous cacophony of church bells ringing. In San Francisco, we start in early morning darkness, run a few miles of fabled waterfront, and then turn to see the sun rising on the Golden Gate Bridge against a cloudless summer sky, a sight made more wondrous by knowing that within thirty minutes, we will be running across the bridge. In Duluth, Minnesota, we run for miles along a sparkling, early morning Lake Superior shorefront, which feels more like ocean than lake. And in my adopted hometown of Minneapolis, on the first weekend of every October, we are enraptured by stunning fall colors as we circle the beautiful city lakes.

Running marathons also provides an unexpected bonus—the opportunity to help others. Following my early New York City Marathon experiences, I am forever moved by the courage of disabled athletes competing in marathons. In the initial phase of my fifty-after-fifty program, I take the plunge and volunteer as an Achilles International guide, accompanying disabled runners in the New York City Marathon. These are the best kinds of volunteer experiences—

satisfying, enriching, and inspiring.

My top running thrill, without a doubt, is participating in the Boston Marathon. It's the oldest American marathon, and competing in Boston carries great prestige among runners. Having grown up close to Boston, I view it as one of the sporting world's most iconic events. I never dreamed I would run it, partly because I was not a runner, and partly because even among runners, it seemed like an unattainable goal. Boston has stringent qualifying standards, and for a recreational runner like me, it's tough to qualify. Gaining entry is to attain the Holy Grail; it's the gold standard of marathon events. I narrowly miss twice before qualifying for the first time at the age of fifty. I run my first of many Boston Marathons shortly after returning from Italy. There is the added thrill that Kate and I run it together. She is also a first-time qualifier.

Bostonians love this event and are the consummate hosts, treating marathon runners like rock stars. Everywhere one goes—restaurants, shops, public transportation—people are solicitous and flattering. Touring the runners' expo the day before race day leaves me feeling giddy. It is a massive market—noisy, crowded, and joyous—with hundreds of kiosks. Merchants sell clothing, technology gadgets, nutritional products, and travel experiences. I often bump into Minneapolis-based runners that I haven't seen in years. The whole experience is Woodstock for runners.

The socializing is continuous, and it centers around what have become traditional food events with different friend groups: Saturday night pasta in the Italian North End, Sunday breakfast at a hole-in-the-wall diner in Beacon Hill, post-race dinner at a favorite seafood place, and finally a solo trip to Ben & Jerry's, where I have three massive scoops on a cone and send selfies to my kids.

Then there's that little detail, squeezed in on a Monday morning, of running the race. It's a deceptively difficult course, and the second half is a killer. My running performances in Boston are generally forgettable, but I've also learned that marathon experiences are often about much more than running.

Done! Crossing the finish line, especially at Boston, is a powerful feeling of relief and accomplishment. I retrieve my checked bag and slowly walk the mile back to my rented apartment. An hour later, I am luxuriating in one of life's post-marathon pleasures—a long, hot shower. Relaxed and looking forward to a celebratory dinner with friends, my mind is buzzing with happiness-inducing endorphins. I feel great. As I slowly get dressed, I casually pick up my phone.

What? In the last fifteen minutes, I received twenty-five text messages. I've never received twenty-five messages *in a day*. Most are from friends and family, and some are from numbers I don't even recognize. As I read them, I go into a state of high alert. I've been here before.

"Art, are you okay? Call me ASAP!"

"Dad, call me! I need to hear from you!"

"What happened?"

"Where are you? Were you near the finish line?"

"Are you safe?"

"Did you finish? Have you heard from any of our friends?"

"I just heard the news. Are you in Boston? Did you run today?"

What???? I pop open my laptop and see the news headlines: "Marathon Horror," "Explosions at the Finish Line," "Area on Lockdown," "Heavy Casualties at Marathon," "Explosions' Cause Unknown." I am bewildered, thinking back to the exuberant finish line scene I had just experienced. As I scan the stories, I become aware of the unrelenting sound of ambulances. *Why did I not notice that before?*

The tone of my telephone conversation with Kate is eerily familiar. "Art, are you okay?" she anxiously asks. "This looks like a terrorist attack. Please be smart! Stay safe! If it's terrorists, they're still out there. Please stay close to your apartment tonight. Don't go out to any place with crowds! Promise me you won't go out!"

"I'm fine, I'm fine. I'm not close to the finish line area. I'm fine. I'll cancel my dinner plans. Please don't worry."

I go down the list and return messages and calls. This is happening in real-time, and the horror is sinking in with the breaking news. No one fully understands what is going on. One work colleague I call observes that I have close-up experience at three high-profile terror-ist events: the World Trade Center bombing in 1993, 9/11, and now this. She awkwardly jokes that she will keep her distance from me in the future.

I finally reach Susan, one of my runner friends. She completed the race one minute ahead of the bombs going off and recounts a horrific scene in the finish area. She is traumatized, but thankfully she and all of our other friends and their families are safely account-ed for. Deciding to stay close to home, I tell her it will be best for me to not join our friends for dinner.

My apartment is in a residential section of Boston's South End. I'm starving and finally go out for dinner later to a bar across the street. It's packed, and the atmosphere is electric. Everyone has a story to tell and is hungry for more information. Facts are rapidly emerging: two bombs went off in areas crowded with fans near the finish line; there were multiple fatalities and casualties, although no one has reliable numbers; there is no public confirmation yet how this happened, although terrorism is widely suspected; and if it was a terrorist attack, the terrorists are still at large. That last point has everyone on edge. Rumors are flying.

The guy next to me just came from a nearby hospital where he was working. "It was really shocking. There were so many people who came in on ambulances. It was nuts. I've worked at the hospital for twenty years, and I've never seen anything like this."

One year later, there's discernable pre-race nervousness. Still, Bos-tonians show their character for the tough, determined way they re-spond in the marathon bombing's aftermath. There's no way this will change anybody's race plans. We'll just be smart about it. We know that a public sports event of this stature, conducted over twenty-six miles and viewed by hundreds of thousands of fans, is a potential "soft" target. Anyone can be vulnerable—fans, runners, anyone. It's a popular conversation topic among runners, friends, and families. Security is exceptionally tight, even for the runners themselves. Runners advise their families to stay away from the finish-line area where crowds can be particularly dense. We discuss running the center of the course and staying away from the crowded sidelines.

Once we start running, we know that it will be a special day. The weather is glorious, and Bostonians come out like never before to cheer. The crowds at both the New York City and the Boston Marathons are always large and noisy, but I never experienced numbers or enthusiasm like this. Runners ride a wave of excitement, civic pride, and thunderous cheers as we are treated like special guests at a twenty-six-mile-long party. It's positively exhilarating. *Boston Strong* becomes the city's tagline, and for good reason.

It's for opportunities like this that I run marathons.

17

You Have the Power!

'Tis the gift to be simple, 'tis the gift to be free,
'tis the gift to come down where we ought to be,
And when we find ourselves in the place just right,
'twill be in the valley of love and delight.
—Joseph Brackett, "Simple Gifts"

As my new post-corporate life takes shape, some things are going very well. I am grateful to have more family time, my marathon running program is exceeding expectations, and I'm developing my social network. But professionally, even a couple years after leaving Ameriprise, I still feel at loose ends. I was discouraged by my networking meeting with John a year earlier and have since shied away from the nonprofit leadership idea. I try to keep an open mind, continue to experiment, stay flexible, and be opportunistic. *This is just part of the journey,* I tell myself.

I wonder whether or not teaching is my true calling. It would make perfect sense, given my parental role models and emerging preferences. I've been at it for nearly two years but am still unconvinced. While engaging with students, sharing experiences, and exploring ideas is enjoyable, something's missing.

As I continue sorting it out, a recruiter calls for the Twin Cities Rise (TCR) President & CEO position. TCR is a medium-sized nonprofit that provides work-skills training and job placement for the long-term and chronically unemployed. African American men with multiple barriers to employment, such as criminal and addiction histories, are the target population served, although TCR's doors are open to anybody needing help.

I received a call for this job a year earlier and wasn't interested. It was right around the time that John threw cold water on the idea of leading a nonprofit. Now I listen more intently. Timing is everything, and I am feeling more inclined to consider it.

The more I learn about the program's unconventional approach and high impact, the more interested I become. It emphasizes that healthy behaviors, starting with self-awareness, self-respect, and personal accountability, are the single most important factors for employment success. It developed a "personal empowerment" training model in conjunction with a well-known clinical psychologist that helps to instill those healthy behaviors. TCR's holistic focus on individuals' personal development sets it apart from conventional work-skills-focused programs, and this appeals to me.

I have nagging questions, though. Do I want to give up my flexible lifestyle and all the possibilities that could come from it? And what about the job itself? The mission and model sound great, but day-to-day, I know the reality—nonprofit leaders are fundraisers. Do I really want to make a living by asking other people for money, no matter how noble the cause? I thought I knew the answer. Now I am not sure.

Seated in a small, drab, windowless conference room, I stare across the table at the five middle- and late-middle-aged members of the Board's search committee. All are successful corporate organizational leaders. Two lead human resource departments for large companies. I feel five sets of eyes staring at me. No one is smiling or even feigning pleasantries. They are sizing me up. *What am I doing here?* They seem to share that thought. This is already uncomfortable, and we haven't even started. Once we start, the questions reflect their underlying skepticism.

"Let's see, Art, you're white, suburban, a former corporate businessman, and you have no chief executive experience. What makes you think you can lead TCR?"

"Art, we serve poor, mostly African American men, and we are staffed primarily by Black people. What have you done to demonstrate that you can lead effectively here?

"Hmm, I don't see that you've fundraised before. We need our CEO to raise $3 million annually. How are you going to do that?"

"What's your experience running human services programs?"

All good questions, and I am ready for them. Well, I am ready for most of them.

I speak extensively about my leadership experiences and results at American Express. "Leadership skills are universal," I respond. "I led large organizations for many years, and I understand the value of strong leadership. I know how to listen, communicate, connect, motivate, build teams, create healthy organizational culture, give feedback, make decisions, set ambitious goals, hold people accountable, and get results."

Referring to TCR's clients, I continue. "It doesn't matter to me who they are, what their life experience is, or where they are in life. I resonate with TCR's personal empowerment model. It's about helping people develop the skills so they can reach their potential. These are universal principles, and they relate to all people. Everyone has goals. We all also have fears, personal demons, and multiple barriers that get in the way."

They are staring, trying hard to figure out if I really can connect to TCR's mission. I imagine that they're thinking, *Does this guy get it?*

I do get it. I know that. Relating well to other people, regardless of their backgrounds, has never been an issue for me. *It's not complicated—people are people.* It also is not easy to explain.

I talk about my parents, how I was raised, and the core values I was taught. I describe growing up in New London's diverse community and its lasting impact. After recounting my New London experience, one of the committee members smiles and says, "Art, from the sounds of it, I'd swear we grew up in the same city."

"Really? Where did you grow up, David?" I ask.

"Youngstown, Ohio," he replies.

"Well, no, but I think you get my point."

"Yup, I get it." And he smiles.

While the committee is focusing on whether I connect with TCR's mission and clientele, I am having a different concern. I cannot shake the message from my networking meeting a year earlier: avoid leading a nonprofit unless you want to spend every day asking people for money. I have two powerful fears: that I will hate the job because of the big fundraising requirement and that I will fail. I am at a loss to satisfactorily address these worries. I have never done this before. It's a risk, but I'm feeling motivated by the challenge. *Maybe this is a risk I need to take.*

I allow myself a distraction and flash back two weeks earlier. A different recruiter contacted me about running a wealthy family's business office. I wasn't looking for this or any job, but it sounded too good to be true: an easy, well-paying, low-stress role working for a family with a reputation for integrity and kindness. Unlike the TCR position, this one was well inside my comfort zone. The interview confirmed and strengthened my initial positive impressions.

Now here I am interviewing for the TCR leadership role. They are clearly skeptical about me. For different reasons, I'm skeptical about me too. *Why am I considering this?* The other job would be a breeze by comparison.

Two weeks later, I pick Max up at school, and I am excited to share my news. He opens the car door and drops his impossibly stuffed backpack onto my car's passenger seat. Then he slides his thin, six-foot-tall, fifteen-year-old frame into the seat while simultaneously shoving his backpack to the floor, all in one well-coordinated motion.

"Hey, Max, how was your day?"

"Hey, Dad, my day was good. You?"

"Good," I say, and I pause for a second. "Hey, I had a big day!"

"What happened?"

"Remember I told you I was interviewing for a couple of jobs?"

"Yeah, the family office job and the one at TCR, right?"

"Yes. Well, today I got offers for *both* of them!"

"Wow, that's awesome, Dad!" he enthusiastically cries. A couple seconds pass, he turns away, hesitates, and then asks, "But wait, didn't you say that you decided not to work for anyone full-time and that you wanted to continue teaching?"

"Yeah, I did. But I've been thinking more about that. I'm getting ready to move on from teaching. Both of these new jobs seem interesting. I'm ready to go back to work full-time."

He pauses, processing this information. "So what are you gonna do?"

"I don't know. Here's the deal. The family office job is a dream job. It's running a business office of ten people for a wealthy family, so I'd be handling their investments, trusts, insurance, charitable giving, that kind of thing. It pays well, just like a high-level corporate job. The hours would be reasonable, and with my financial background, I'm a good fit. The best part is the family is very nice. They reached out to me and made me feel welcome, almost like I'm already part of the family. I am feeling valued before I even start there."

"That sounds *great*, Dad. What about the TCR job?"

"It's completely different. I'd be running a larger organization that works with very poor people who are chronically unemployed. TCR helps them get back on their feet and to find good jobs. So it would be sort of like running a job-skills training and placement program, but only for people who have had rough lives."

"What kinds of rough lives?"

"Incarceration, addiction, unstable housing; it really runs the gamut. Max, we have such cloistered lives. We're talking about a completely different world here. This would be hard work. I'd have to do a lot of fundraising too, which is something I've never done before. It's an opportunity to have a real impact, but I have no idea if I'd be any good at it. It also doesn't pay well."

We drive several minutes in silence, both of us absorbing this information and contemplating the possibilities. We pull up to a traffic light as it turns red. I turn to Max and say, "So, what do you think?"

He turns his head to face me, looks me in the eye, and softly says, "Dad, I'd be so proud of you if you take the TCR job."

Living more generously is something I am trying to do. It doesn't always come naturally. I uncharacteristically take the riskier path, have my OSM, and take the TCR job. I am all-in, ready to give it 100 percent. *I'll figure out the fundraising piece*, I think. *I'll do whatever I have to do to make it work.* The teaching experiment is over.

"Your life is a theater," asserts Renee, TCR's extraordinary Personal Empowerment instructor. Two weeks on the new job, I am taking our signature classroom program, excited to experience it shoulder-to-shoulder with our new client cohort.

"You're on the stage, and everyone you know is in the audience," she continues. "You decide who should sit in the front row, who gets moved to the back, and who has to leave altogether. This is the first step in taking control of your life. People who are a positive influence sit in the front. They're the ones you want to see and hear from. They're the ones who affirm your value; they're the ones who affirm that you're lovable, important, and valuable; and they're the ones who are going to help you. Then there are those negative voices—the ones that tempt you to make bad decisions, the ones that drag you down, the ones that bring out your worst—you move them to the back of your theater, or maybe you push them out completely. You don't want to see them or hear them."

My classmates are spellbound, and so am I. Renee has a commanding presence, her words having raw power. I later learn, and am not surprised, that on weekends, she is a preacher in a local church.

She continues, "This is the first step in personal empowerment—learning that you have power. You can control your life. You have choices. You are responsible for you. Empowerment starts with self-awareness, and the awareness that you have personal power. Most of you here feel unempowered. You feel like victims. I know you do. I hear it in my coaching sessions. You feel like other people control your lives. You feel powerless. Well, I'm telling you that's not true. You can take control. You have the power! Start with your relationships. You have the power to decide who sits in the front row of your theater and who needs to leave. Who is going to support your success? Who will affirm your value? Who will bring out the best in you? And who brings out the worst? Who tempts you to make bad decisions? Who is going to drag you back down? You have the power to decide."

A couple hours later, I am walking near the office, and I spot two of our new clients at an outdoor café. Jerry and Richard are soaking up the July sun, and I join them.

"How did you guys like our first Personal Empowerment class?" I ask.

"Yeah, it was good," replies Jerry. "That Renee is somethin' else."

"Yeah," Richard agrees.

Jerry and Richard, I learn, share a room at a halfway house. They are middle-aged men whose lives were derailed by alcoholism, and neither have held a full-time job in years.

"You know, that 'life is a theater' story really hit me," Jerry continues. "I was just thinking about some of those guys at our house. It's hard to be around them. Renee's right, I need to wall them off from my life. They're a bad influence."

"Yeah," Richard interjects. "Some of those guys are going backward, and we're trying to go forward. We can't be hangin' around with them no more."

It's six months later, and I'm staring out the frosty windows at the bare, commercial expanse of Minneapolis's Washington Avenue North. It's a gray day, but I barely notice. I don't see the winter street scene—the stark, industrial warehouse-style low-rise apartment building across the way, or people exiting their cars, hunkered down against the wind as they navigate snowbanks between the street and the sidewalk. I don't see anything. My mind is off on its own whimsical journey, and my vision is imbued with light, possibilities, and hope.

I also have a sense of urgency about the hours immediately ahead. I canceled classes for the day. It seemed like the right thing to do. I am still expecting a full house of clients and staff for the event. It's an historic day.

"Let's go, Ed," I implore. "I have no patience for this! The show starts in an hour!" I am anxious. Ed, our IT guy, is still trying to figure out how to project the television picture on the big screen. Our front-desk receptionist is helping me as we feverishly set up several dozen folding chairs in a stadium style.

My staff are all happily in disbelief. They have been for two months following the presidential election. The prevailing attitude is "Pinch me. Is this really happening?"

Today is January 20, 2009, and in an hour Barack Obama will be inaugurated as the forty-fourth President, and our first Black President. I am excited to be a witness to history, especially to experience the moment in this space and with this group of people.

The classroom slowly fills up with clients, as staff members warmly greet them. I am forever awed by my colleagues. They are servant leaders who do the hardest work every day. They provide hope to the hopeless, strength to the powerless, and a path forward to people who are unskilled, formerly incarcerated, homeless, recovering from addiction, chronically unemployed, and marginalized. They intuitively know how to strike the right balance between compassionate support and holding people firmly accountable to do better. They instinctively understand the struggle—not long ago, many of them were the ones struggling. As program graduates, they are now role models—people in difficult situations who assertively changed by taking control of their lives. Now, they are the Givers, having made their own redemptive journeys.

In theory, I am their leader. In reality, I am humbled in their presence, and I draw daily inspiration from their courage, wisdom, and strength. They don't realize it, but they are role models to me as well as to our clients. In their teaching, coaching, and inspiring, they often remind me of this Booker T. Washington quote: "Success is to be measured not so much by the position that one has reached in life as by the obstacles which he has overcome."

The ceremony starts with a stirring musical touch, as Yo-Yo Ma and Itzhak Perlman play an elegant, soulful rendition of the Shaker melody "Simple Gifts." It seems fitting, and I already feel emotions welling up. Barack Obama finally takes the oath of office and approaches the podium for his inaugural address. He rouses the record-setting crowd, invoking his vision of our country's core values—honesty, hard work, courage, fair play, tolerance, curiosity, loyalty, and patriotism. He shares a vision about how great we can be when we seek common ground with those different from us and when we open our hearts to those in need. I am moved by his eloquence and grace.

Looking around the room, I take a mental snapshot so that I will never forget. It's a rapt audience. Our clients and my staff colleagues are tight-lipped and expressionless, absorbing the moment, appearing to appreciate its significance but saying little. I am surprised that there is no observable emotion. I can only guess what everyone is thinking.

Their comments afterward express great pride and even a state of awe. But with the ceremony's end, I also know that our clients will be heading outside, waiting in the freezing cold for public transportation, and going home to poorly heated apartments, dysfunctional relationships, physical and mental health challenges, and all of the other stresses of lives in deep poverty. I try to empathize, but the reality is that I cannot imagine. I will go home later to my comfortable suburban house and a supportive, loving family.

We set a high success standard for our clients: they must complete the one-year training program, get a full-time job, and keep it for a year. Only then do they graduate. More often than not, we fail, experiencing far more dropouts than successes. Program expectations are high; that is our ethos. Our persistent failure rate keeps us focused and humble, determined to do better.

Successes, while outnumbered by failures, are still remarkable. Our graduates' stories of personal transformation astonish me: the homeless guy who woke up in a vacant parking lot, saw an old, larger-than-life billboard of himself as an athletic star, and decided "enough is enough," and then, with TCR's help, successfully became a personal coach and role model for his family and community; the woman who was drug-dependent, suicidally depressed, and couldn't hold a job, who was literally talked off the ledge by a TCR coach, got the mental health and drug counseling supports she needed, and became an office administrator and model employee; and the guy who was in and out of jail for a decade because of alcohol-fueled fist fights, who embraced the emotional regulation lessons of personal empowerment training, learned to control his alcohol consumption and anger, and became a high school athletic coach and community leader. There are hundreds of other inspiring stories like these.

TCR's reputation grows across the state and nationally. We quantify the return on investment to taxpayers, showing how TCR—by training the long-term unemployed to get and keep jobs, get off public-support programs, stay out of the criminal justice system, and become taxpaying citizens—reduces everyone's tax burden. A small army of bipartisan local, state, and national politicians, from the Twin Cities' Democratic mayors to the state's Tea Party Republicans to our national representatives like Senators Amy Klobuchar and Al Franken, and Representatives Keith Ellison, Betty McCollum, and John Kline, provide vocal support. Most of them visit and participate in a personal empowerment class. Ashoka, the leading international advocate for social entrepreneurship, selects TCR as one of five organizations from nearly one thousand global applicants for its annual social innovation prize. I participate as a guest on a national public radio news program focusing on effective anti-poverty programs. Work-skills training programs in Chicago and San Francisco call seeking advice. The U.S. Department of Labor expresses interest in designing a national demonstration project based on the TCR model.

At a more grassroots level, *Minnesota Monthly* selects TCR as one of the top fifty employers in the state of Minnesota. We are the top-rated social service nonprofit. Creating a healthy, empowering organizational culture is fundamental to our success and is a strong personal priority. This recognition is especially affirming. I am enriched by this experience, even as I am, at times, overwhelmed by its challenges.

"Hi Kris, it's been awhile!" I say, as I take my seat at the outdoor café. It's three years after President Obama's inauguration, and it's a perfect late-spring day—sunny, warm, and pleasant. It's the kind of day when Minnesotans eagerly take a restaurant's *al fresco* option. Kris is a friend and former American Express colleague. She, like me, left the company and transitioned into a new, service-oriented chapter of life a couple years earlier. She also helps at TCR by volunteering as a mock interviewer and a fundraising event planner. She is a friend, colleague, and trusted sounding board.

"I know! Great to see you, Art," she says with a smile, responding to my greeting.

"So," she continues, diving right in to conversation as I settle into my seat, "how's TCR going these days? Let's see, you've been at it now for how many years?" Eyes sparkling, she asks, "Are you loving every minute of it?" It is a leading question, sincerely asked. It's clear she expects my response to be gushingly affirmative.

Her presumption is a common one, particularly amongst my former corporate colleagues. The logic goes like this: after having a long corporate career where we worked for bottom-line-focused shareholders and ego-driven leaders, it must feel wonderful every day to serve a different, more resonant purpose and to have a direct, meaningful impact on the people in our community who are in greatest need. What could be better than that?

This view is precisely why I made this career choice. My reaction, though, is quite contrary. She inadvertently pushes a button. I think, *Are you kidding? I'm miserable! I've got fundraising headaches, staff performance issues, frustrations with government funding bureaucracy, and insomnia over the prospect of laying people off. Do you think that running a service organization, starved for cash but unwilling to turn people away, is all sweetness and light?* These immediate thoughts rapidly swirl, but I keep my mouth shut as I contemplate an answer.

She looks at me with an expectant smile as I collect my thoughts, still holding my tongue. Taking a deep breath, I gain control and recall my good fortune and leadership role. I smile, knowing her positive intent. "Yes," I acknowledge, "I am lucky to be here." Stopping to contemplate additional thoughts, I hesitate, frown, and then say, "Can I share some day-to-day issues that are bothering me?"

Continuing to smile, she replies, "Yes, of course. What's up?"

I depend on many people for counsel and support. Kate is tops among them. Her wisdom and big, philanthropic heart are always present as a guiding light. She also volunteers in many ways, once again role modeling what true community leadership looks like. There are also hundreds of other volunteers who provide invaluable help. Most importantly, my exceptional group of colleagues is the most inspiring team I've had on any job.

As for fundraising, I am proud to represent TCR, promote its successes, and invite others to invest in our community. I take the approach that I'm not selling; rather, I am giving prospective donors the opportunity to help others and build a stronger, more inclusive community. It works out much better than I could have hoped. While it's not my natural gift, I grow into the role. Our annual fundraising outcomes consistently improve during my tenure.

It also wears me down. I feel the daily burden of meeting ambitious financial targets to support our clients and staff. With our aggressive fundraising targets and the challenges of serving inexorably growing community needs, my insomnia never goes away. For the second time in my professional life, I am feeling burnout.

When I started at TCR, I set a personal goal of staying for three to five years. After nearly six years, I am now in my late-fifties and am ready to move on. Move on to what? I'm not sure, but it's time for a break and then to prepare for whatever comes next. There's more that I want to do in this world. I resign and adopt a "we'll see" attitude.

After leaving TCR, I scratch a personal itch and enroll in a full-time, two-year culinary arts program, training to become a professional chef. I have no intention of becoming a chef. I'm in it simply to learn new skills and to have some fun until my next "serious" endeavor. It's a welcome break. Life is different when my biggest worry is whether or not my hollandaise sauce will properly emulsify, or if class will end in time for me to grab leftovers from the French pastry class next door. I am thirty years older than my next oldest classmate. I have a blast, enjoy the moment, and know that a new chapter will begin soon enough.

PART IV

Making Sense of It

18

REFLECTION

If on September 10, 2001, someone had asked me what made my life special, I would have cited many gifts—a stable and loving family, career opportunities, good health, and more. I was grateful for a very good life.

If I was further asked what made my life unique, or inspiring, I would have struggled to answer. My priorities were clear—work and family, family and work—there was nothing else. There wasn't time for anything else. It was neither unique nor inspiring, but it worked for me. At least for the time being.

I would also have acknowledged that I lived squarely inside my comfort zone, rarely venturing out. That was a choice, a safe choice, driven by a strong sense of responsibility to family and career, as well as my naturally risk-averse instincts. I chose not to test my limits, not to challenge my assumptions, and not to meaningfully engage in the world outside of family and work. I felt no compulsion to disrupt a benign status quo; the thought barely registered. Social approbation that came with steady career growth and a comfortable home life, not to mention the security of a growing paycheck, provided more than enough affirmation to stay on this safe track.

Then came 9/11. In its immediate aftermath, I habitually read a section in the New York Times called "Portraits in Grief." Each portrait was a personal profile of someone who died from the 9/11 attacks. There were dozens that described middle-aged, professional dads who were dedicated family men, who worked hard, who had long commutes into New York City from their suburban homes, and who coached their kids' soccer and baseball teams on weekends.

Those portraits described me.

One hundred Art Bermans died that day. Or maybe two hundred. Or three hundred. Or more. Those portraits broke my heart.

They also shook me up. I knew those guys. I saw them on my commuter train, at my favorite coffee shop, on the youth soccer sidelines, and at my kids' school. I saw one in the mirror every day. If processing this information could be likened to a geological event, the tectonic plates beneath my surface shifted massively. And like that type of geological event, its impact was not initially apparent, nor was its potential for long-term disruption at all understood. But it triggered something.

Multiple experiments and many years later, I began to understand how I wanted to change and what drove me—what I was missing, what more I wanted, what I had to do, and why. Change began when I pushed myself outside of my comfort zone. It was not an easy step for a preternaturally cautious guy, a guy who feared failure. But a new, stronger foundation eventually formed, and clarity followed.

It began with a post-9/11 family move to Minneapolis. I stretched for a professional goal that was initially unattainable. Once finally within reach, I didn't want it. My corporate career had to slowly crumble and then collapse—the impact of those continuously shifting tectonic plates—before I could move on. Sometimes experiments fail. In my conventional, controlled life, this was a pretty spectacular failure. It was also for the best. Wiser for the experience, I moved forward without regret.

Winging off to Italy was a lark, meant to be no more than a whimsical bridge to the next phase of a temporarily disrupted business career. That trip's timing, it turns out, was perfect. La dolce vita's impact, obscured in the moment by the fuzzy warmth of family travel, was lasting. For the first time in my adult life, I had the gift of time. I spent it with my favorite people in a most agreeable place. Oh what a gift it was!

It was the simple, day-to-day pleasures: sipping morning caffé lattes in a sun-drenched piazza with Kate, followed by meandering trips through the food markets; chauffeuring the girls to and from school, with playground time at the end of the day; exploring Florence on foot with Max and feeling a sense of gratitude and awe every time we walked together through those streets; learning a new language *in situ* and making it a fun, playful experience; savoring *al fresco* family dinners, capped off with passeggiata and gelato; acquiring a taste for the local Chianti Classico, rationalizing it as a heart-healthy habit; tripping my imagination regularly, as we all experienced boundless cultural wonders and beauty; and with each day's end, the simple pleasure of racing the girls up an impossibly long stairway, our laughter bouncing loudly off of the centuries-old stone walls. Italy brought a close family even closer together. We shared experiences that opened our minds, filled our senses, nourished our souls, warmed our hearts, and titillated our taste buds.

It also rewired my thinking. It began my own rebirth, fittingly set where Europe's Renaissance began. Leaving for Italy, I still clung to a conventional personal narrative, dictating a narrow set of choices that responsible professionals make. I would simply take a respite before reengaging in the corporate workforce. That plan vaporized within weeks of our return.

Contemplating how to get my career back on track, I realized that the whole point was to jump the well-worn track and create new ones. Not knowing exactly what that meant, I experimented. My internal compass guided me toward satisfying three personal goals that I felt but could not yet articulate—to live more courageously, to live more generously, and to live with greater intention.

The community leadership roles I found were on the right path, and they came at the right time. In my early fifties, for the first time, I was able to more holistically combine personal, family, community, and professional values. That is what I had been searching for.

An embedded, selfish motivation continues to guide this choice; I feel as though I give generously, but I get far more in return. Community organizations where I've volunteered or worked, such as

TCR, bring me back to my roots. Many boyhood friends didn't have my good fortune of an emotionally supportive and stable home life. In some ways, life has come full circle. My TCR colleagues overcame much higher barriers than I ever faced, and they did it with strength and dignity.

Several months after leaving TCR, I took a position as an interim executive director for a large faith-based service organization. At the job interview, an ordained pastoral leader observed that it seems I am "called to service." He asked me if that is true. Oddly enough, the question threw me. Not being religiously observant, I do not think in those terms. I described what motivated me in secular terms, studiously avoiding religious references and the idea of being "called" by a higher power. After I answered, he smiled and said, "Yes, Art, you are making my point. You are called to serve others."

My first TCR Personal Empowerment lesson—choose carefully who you allow into your life—resonates even more with time. I better understand the profound impact that relationships, whether they're with family, friends, work colleagues, clients, or even random interactions with strangers, have on my mood and outlook. "Life is a theater" is TCR's first lesson in self-awareness, in taking responsibility, and in acknowledging the influences of others in your life.

Thanks to Mom and Dad's legacy, and the life that Kate and I built together, my theater starts in the most likely of places—family, including extended family. All of my family members embrace those qualities that my parents role-modeled so well—love, empathy, integrity, humility, grace, humor, curiosity, and many more. Family has always been my source of strength and my emotional safety net. We spend our lifetimes investing in each other. Nothing matters more.

19. Gold Medals

We don't grow older. We grow riper.

—Pablo Picasso

Now in my mid-sixties, I am transitioning into a new life stage. I often reflect on how one's outlook changes with age and circumstance. Some things, like core values, will never change. Mom and Dad taught us well about those non-negotiable principles—family's central role, the importance of contributing to our communities, and faithful adherence to those values.

What I am learning, though, is that attitude evolves. Living with intention becomes more critical with advancing age. Life doesn't get easier, and tough decisions lie ahead. In Arthur Brooks' Aspen Ideas Festival presentation, he describes a formula for how to find happiness and grace in life's later stages, despite the inevitable decline that accompanies aging. One key rule is to do the opposite of Dylan Thomas's message from his epic poem, "Do Not Go Gentle into That Good Night." In that poem, the author advises his dying father to "rage, rage against the dying of the light." This advice, according to Brooks, is what many highly successful people do, and it inevitably leads to frustration and unhappiness in older age. We will all experience decline in life's second half, so it's best to accept it rather than fight it. For me, this message of "take what life gives you with grace, gratitude, and good humor" is well-received.

But it's not that simple. Facing diminishing capacity, how do we accept decline while also continuing to grow in other ways? How do we keep our spirits fresh while also nurturing our minds and bodies? I am fortunate to have many later-stage role models in my family and network of close friends—lifelong learners, engaged grandparents, contributing community members, intrepid travelers, voracious readers, dedicated athletes, talented artists, fabulous cooks—people who still choose to live life to its fullest while also adjusting expectations with equanimity.

My lifelong love for sports provides a unique perspective, capturing many of these lessons. Athletic competition is a natural and stark laboratory for how performance diminishes with age. Decline, often steep decline, is inevitable. I am experiencing that in my day-to-day running, and I have been for years. Yet I don't have to look far for constructive ways to deal with that. These lessons often come from seemingly random, even mundane encounters with someone special that leave me feeling enlightened, enriched, and inspired.

At the age of sixty, my team qualifies for the three-on-three basketball competition at the National Senior Games. These Games are multiday, multi-sport events that take place semi-annually and that are loosely modeled as a kind of Olympic Games for aging athletes.

I'm waiting in line to check into my Birmingham, Alabama, hotel. I casually turn around and see a tiny, striking woman with short, platinum-blonde hair, bright-red lipstick, and deep facial wrinkles, resplendent in a luminous purple tracksuit and top-of-the-line runners' shoes. *My God, this woman's an athlete? She must be eighty-five years old!* She is all smiles.

"Hi, are you here to compete in the Senior Games?" I ask.

"Yes, my name is June. And who are you?" she responds with a friendly southern drawl, a welcoming smile, and an extended hand.

"Hi June, I'm Art," and we share a warm handshake. "I'm also here for the Games. What sport do you play?" *Track—that couldn't be it, could it? Swimming? Table tennis? What else could it be?* I have no idea.

"Shuffleboard," she proudly asserts. "I'm here to defend my gold medals from the last four Games!"

"Wow, that's awesome, June! Congratulations!" I enthusiastically gush.

I ponder her answer, and I have to ask the question. "June, how old are you?" This is a question that senior athletes often ask each other, as we are always curious. The question is never unwelcome. Senior athletes are proud to participate in competitive sports despite advancing age and are forthcoming in sharing this information.

"Ninety-four," she replies with a radiant grin and a twinkling eye.

"It's you again!" says Mary, greeting me with a glowing smile.

She is one of the first people I met at the Senior Games a couple days ago, and ever since that meeting, we keep randomly crossing paths. She is a sixty-eight-year-old long-distance runner with straight, shoulder-length white hair, a deep tan, and a lean, runner's build. She is chronically, infectiously cheerful.

"How did it go this morning?" I ask, remembering that she ran in the ten-kilometer road race today.

"I'm happy," she replies, all smiles. "I came in dead last, but I didn't poop in my pants, and I finished strong."

"Ha ha, congratulations, I guess! Here's to setting ambitious goals!" And we both laugh. "So, where are you off to now?"

"I told my grandchildren I came in first place. So I'm gonna go to Target and buy a gold medal. Then I can prove to them that I won."

Senior athletes have a knack for defining success so that we are always winners.

Another senior athlete had the starring role in my most memorable marathon experience. His was the grittiest athletic performance I ever witnessed, and I had the good fortune to help him set a record at the 2016 New York City Marathon. Fittingly, it was in the wondrous city that holds so many personal memories.

In one sweeping motion, I sit up with a start and toss the covers aside. I swing my legs around, sit on the edge of the bed, and grab my phone. 4:15 a.m. *Was I sleeping? Did I get any sleep at all?* Nights before a marathon are always spent in back-and-forth states of light sleep and barely conscious wakefulness.

My brain is involuntarily racing. During the night, we switched from daylight saving to standard time, contributing to an enveloping angst. *Did my phone clock adjust automatically and show the right time?* I think it did, but I'm groggy and can't really think straight. *Why is the clock on the hotel nightstand showing 5:15? Did I just miss my five o'clock bus? Holy cow, I am confused! Slow down!*

I check my phone again. No messages. If I was late, I would have gotten a "Where are you?" message by now. I turn on the television, and it shows the time as 4:20. I am still in a brain fog. I call the hotel's front desk clerk, and he confirms that it's twenty minutes past four. Finally calm, I make a cup of coffee, chomp down several slices of bread, get dressed, pack for the day, and hit the road.

I stroll briskly up Manhattan's Fifth Avenue toward the New York City Public Library, where I will meet my two marathon companions for the day: ninety-six-year-old Jon Mendes and his personal trainer, Tom. We are catching the early bus to the race's Staten Island start. I know it will be a long day. Little do I know what is really in store.

I first met the larger-than-life nonagenarian, Jon Mendes, one year earlier.

"Hi Jon, my name is Art Berman, and . . ."

"What? What? What?" he shouts into the phone. "Give me five minutes to put in my hearing aids and then call back!" He abruptly hangs up.

It's one week before the 2015 New York City Marathon, and this is my first contact with Jon. At the age of ninety-five, and possessing an irrepressible gift of gab, a disarming sense of humor, and an iron constitution, Jon decides he wants to complete a marathon. No stranger to the event, he last completed the full distance at the age of eighty-nine. He wants to finish one more time, feeling that he has something to prove—to himself, to his doubting family, and to the world.

To assist him, he requests a marathon guide from Achilles International, the organization that provides guided support for athletes with disabilities. I am now an Achilles volunteer. From the first time I observed Achilles athletes in Central Park, I was amazed by their commitment and courage. It's an honor to help these athletes beat the odds and complete the distance. This year, I am assigned to support Jon in his quest to complete a marathon. His personal trainer, Tom, will also accompany us.

Our first meeting at the runners' expo confirms what I sensed from our call—Jon is amazing. I am immediately taken by his bubbly, extroverted personality. He talks to everybody, and his effervescence leaves us all smiling. Physically diminutive, he also has an intense presence, a deliberate stride, and a determined air. I am not surprised to learn of his impressive resume—he is a highly decorated ex-Marine airman and veteran of World War II and the Korean War, where he flew with John Glenn and Ted Williams, the Hall of Fame baseball player. He later earned a Harvard MBA and had a successful Wall Street career.

Jon did extraordinarily well the first year I accompanied him, completing 16 of the race's 26.2 miles. As we came off of the Queensboro Bridge into Manhattan, the race's sag wagon bus, shadowed by a long caravan of police cars and emergency service vehicles, signaled that we were dead last among the fifty-thousand runners who began the race. It took us seven hours to get there. Listening to his depleted body and his family's entreaties, he called it a day. I was impressed—sixteen miles is a mind-boggling accomplishment for a ninety-five-year-old man.

Now, nearly one year later and a few weeks prior to the 2016 race, Jon and I reconnect by phone. He wants to try again.

"Art, I know I'll finish this year. That's my goal. I know I can do it!" he asserts confidently. "You're going to help me. And when we get to mile twenty in the Bronx, we're going to take out a bottle of scotch and celebrate."

"That sounds great, Jon. But you know if you have a scotch at mile twenty, you'll never make it out of the Bronx."

"Art, when I was in the Marines, we always carried our fallen comrades off of the battlefield," teasingly suggesting that Tom and I should prepare to carry him out of the Bronx and, I assumed, the final six miles to the finish line.

There is a nervous excitement, even at five in the morning, as Achilles athletes and guides board our Midtown buses to head for the start. The level of activity, and the military precision by which fifty-thousand runners are transported in the wee hours on a Sunday morning, are incredible. As we all settle into our seats, I ask Jon how he is feeling about the day ahead. His face lights up, his deeply recessed eyes sparkle, and his crow's feet deepen.

"Twenty-six at ninety-six. That's what I'm doing today, twenty-six miles at ninety-six years old." No one over the age of ninety-three has ever completed the New York City Marathon, and he is determined to set a new record as its oldest finisher ever. His excitement and confidence are palpable. He is sure that he will make history today. He warmly smiles and repeats the words. "Twenty-six at ninety-six." This will be our mantra for the day.

The bus ride from Midtown Manhattan to Staten Island's start area is a long, slow, and quiet affair. Early morning excitement quickly subsides, and most of us doze off or talk softly. I stir just a little as we motor south on Manhattan's FDR Drive. I face east toward Brooklyn, sleepily admiring the early rising sun over the East River. It is a beautiful and eerily peaceful cityscape, as the low rising sun creates a long line of beautifully silhouetted buildings. It is a small and lovely part of the experience, particularly as I look ahead, knowing that an estimated two million enthusiastically cheering spectators will await us in hours on New York City's streets.

Arriving at the Achilles Athletes village, there is already an electrifying excitement among athletes and guides. The buzz of nervous conversation and laughter is contagious, though there is little time to savor it. The ambulatory Achilles athletes and guides will get a head start before the entire fifty-thousand runner field; we are a slow group. Jon can barely contain himself as we begin our climb up to the Verrazzano Bridge's starting line.

It is a magnificent fall day. There's a clear blue sky, a chill in the air, and a whipping breeze on the bridge's deck. As we line up to start, Jon assertively moves to the front of the assembled runners. The official starter says, "Runners, on your mark, get set . . ." and Jon drops down into a sprinter's crouch. At the sound of "go," to everyone's delight, he springs forward like a world-class runner exploding out of his starter blocks. Tom and I look at each other, eyes dancing and grins widening. We share an unspoken thought: *Jon is feeling it—we have an entertaining day ahead.* Making others laugh, we know, gives Jon great pleasure.

We catch up with him, and I am impressed by how Jon, despite his start-line antics, immediately dials in on his goal. We focus on establishing and maintaining a steady walking pace, which I will track for most of the day.

Here we all are—fifty ambulatory Achilles athletes and guides, walking on the two-mile-long bridge's empty upper deck. It connects Staten Island to Brooklyn and provides a stunning panoramic view of Brooklyn, Manhattan, and New Jersey, though we don't take time to admire it. The wind is howling, causing our windbreakers to loudly crackle. We shout in conversation so that we can hear each other.

The friendly, early arriving Brooklyn crowds respond delightedly as Jon proudly displays his U.S. Marine Corps sweatshirt and baseball cap. With great enthusiasm, he repeatedly greets them with a "Semper Fi, Do or Die, Oorah!" cheer. They salute, smile, and laugh. Throughout the day, Marines and other armed services veterans warmly engage with Jon and share information on where they served. Their parting greetings are always some variation of "God bless you, Jon, and thank you for your service!" It is a continuous stream of uplifting moments.

The crowds give Jon energy; he loves talking and making people smile. In addition to the spectators, he enjoys engaging with the marathon runners as they steadily catch up and pass us in long, continuous waves. They regularly give enthusiastic cheers of their own, occasionally slowing down and turning to get a better look. "How old are you?" many ask.

"Ninety-six!" Jon proudly replies.

"Oh my God, no way!"

Many of the female runners ask for hugs. After one, Jon turns to us and says, "If I had known I'd get this much attention from the ladies, I would have dressed better for the occasion." One asks him for a kiss, and he happily accommodates. Several take pictures. We learned later that Jon's picture was a viral sensation on Snapchat.

To one older woman walker who slowly passes us, he asks, "Do you want to go dancing after the marathon?"

Surprised and amused, she looks over and says, "Sure, I'd love to!"

"By the way, how old are you?" he inquires.

When she replies eighty-five, he shakes his head and says, "I'm sorry, but you're too young for me. I prefer more mature women." And on we go.

Williamsburg's Hasidic Jewish section presents a special challenge for the hyper-social Jon. He is proud of his own Sephardic Jewish ancestral roots. He attempts to engage several Hasidic men in conversation, but they just stare back, effectively ignoring him. We then come upon a large group of teenage Hasidic girls, congregating behind a schoolyard's iron gate. Jon approaches them, and without introduction or hesitation, he starts chanting a Hebrew prayer. "Shema, Yisra'el, Adonai, Elohenu . . ." They look blankly back at him in disbelief, not knowing what to think.

Jon stops in mid-prayer and loudly declares, "I'm Sephardic! I'm Jewish!"

One girl lights up and excitedly asks, "You're Jewish?"

"Yes, I'm Jewish!" he enthusiastically replies.

"He's Jewish!" several of them shout, and they all break out in smiles.

"Yes! And I'm ninety-six years old!"

Their smiles broaden. It makes Jon's day.

Even with all of this socializing, we are able to maintain a steady pace. Tom and I remain vigilant of Jon's physical needs. We are constantly working with him, adjusting his posture, and ticking off our checklist: "Legs? Back? Vision? Water? Bathroom break? Clothes?

Too hot? Are you sweating? Too cold? Are you chilled?" Jon's back stiffens up, and we stop twice, allowing Tom to massage him.

A bigger problem in the early stages is Jon's vision. The sunlight is intense, and we are frequently passing between sun and shade. Jon is unable to adjust his vision to the changing light, and our biggest fear is him stumbling and falling on the uneven pavement. We take turns holding him by the elbow as he puts a hand on the other one's shoulder, making sure he maintains balance.

All things considered, he does remarkably well through the first half. We maintain our pace, and I am amazed as he shows few signs of fatigue. I know it's just a matter of time.

We reach Manhattan at mile sixteen, a major milestone. This is last year's drop-out point. I didn't expect him to make it this far, and Jon is now tiring. The energy-inducing crowds are gone as we are about to enter a new phase. Despite his flagging energy, he remains determined. "Remember, men, twenty-six at ninety-six," he reminds us. He leans more heavily on our arms for support, and we slowly soldier on.

I have mixed feelings at this point. Early on I was thinking, *Wouldn't it be cool if Jon could go the distance*, not really believing that he could, or that it would be such a good idea for him to even try. He is becoming more unsteady by the block, and we still have ten miles to go. My worries grow.

Gallows humor creeps into our conversation. Heading up Manhattan's First Avenue, Jon looks west toward Central Park, just one mile away and where the race will end. He reflects on how easy it would be to take a shortcut across town to the finish area. "I know, I can pull a Rosie Ruiz," he jokes, referring to the woman who was infamously disqualified decades earlier from both the Boston and New York City Marathons for taking subway rides to cut race distance and time.

Jon's family meets us with hot beverages and encouragement—encouragement at the eighteen miles we covered, and encouragement to be sensible and drop out. Jon gratefully accepts a hot tea, but he becomes increasingly agitated with the dropout talk. He has kept a regular patter for hours about finishing and setting a new record. "Twenty-six at ninety-six." Nothing, and nobody, is going to dissuade him.

The conversation takes on a more urgent tone, and his family begs him to stop the madness and to be reasonable. They genuinely fear that he will drop dead from exhaustion if he continues. Quietly observing, I share that concern.

Jon impatiently and angrily cuts it off.

"Stop arguing with me! This is my decision! I'm going!" he shouts. He abruptly turns and continues north on First Avenue. Tom and I scramble to catch up.

It is late afternoon; the sun is setting, and an early evening chill descends. The course is officially closed, the mile markers are taken down, and all of the water stops are reduced to single unattended tables with cups of water. We note, a little jokingly but mostly grimly, that as we move past mile twenty into the Bronx and away from Central Park's finish line, we are committing to the entire race distance. *Are we nuts? He's ninety-six years old and completely exhausted.* There will be no turning back.

Jon is now walking in between us, holding both of us to keep his balance and maintain a slight forward body lean. The tightness of his grip increases, as does the weight he is placing on us. Tom and I switch sides to ease the pressure on our forearms; mine are going numb. I know that tomorrow morning my legs will feel fine but that the soreness will be in my arms and shoulders. Jon continuously loosens and tightens his grip, experimenting with different places to hold on. The position that now works best is when we hold hands, as he rests his forearms heavily on ours, and then we nestle our elbows under his armpits. We aren't carrying him, but we are bearing considerable weight. It is not helpful, either, that I am much taller than Jon, so I walk many miles in a bent posture.

We now have a new concern: getting lost in the Bronx darkness. We strain to see the lightly painted blue line in the middle of the street marking the course, but we can no longer walk in the street because of the freely flowing traffic. Although I have run this course many times, I haven't experienced it in total darkness and without other visual guides. We are navigating on my directional instincts.

We pass a couple of liquor stores, and Jon briefly perks up. "A beer would taste so good right now. I want a beer. Let's stop for a beer."

At first we think he's kidding, and we make light of it. But then he keeps asking. *He's not joking.* We ignore him. I keep waiting for him to ask for a scotch. He never does.

I am chilled to the bone. I dressed totally wrong for this event. This is my fourth marathon as a walker/Achilles guide. I still do not know how to dress appropriately for one: how to stay not too hot and not too cold, how to adjust to changing weather patterns and temperatures over a very long day, and how to do it while following the NYPD's "no backpack" rule for participants—thus limiting the options for carrying extra clothes as a contingency. It's a creativity and resilience test, and I am again failing it.

We navigate the Bronx without incident and cross back into Manhattan at mile twenty-one. It feels like progress, but the biggest test lies ahead. A marathon's last five miles are always the hardest. With our barely shuffling pace, it's hard to fathom covering five blocks, let alone five miles.

We stop every block, as Jon is completely spent. We never sit down. If we do, we know we won't get him back on his feet. At each stop, he catches his breath and we find something for him to lean on, giving his muscles a brief respite. By the time we reach Central Park on Fifth Avenue, we are counting down the blocks . . . 100, 99, 98, 97, 96 . . . As we pass within two blocks of his 94th Street apartment, Jon casts a long look in its direction. I am wondering what he's thinking. *It would be so easy for him to declare victory at twenty-three miles, simply take a left, and go home.* We continue on. I am awed by him. *What an incredibly tough guy!* We turn right into the quiet darkness of Central Park, heading south on Park Drive. We are nearing mile twenty-four.

With less than a mile to go, we trudge up the final stretch on Central Park South. We wonder if the finish line will still be set up and if anyone will be around to mark our finish. It is more than eleven hours since our early morning start. Most runners finished hours ago.

As we approach the finish line, all doubts are dispelled. A few hundred yards from the finish, a *Runner's World* magazine writer stops us, and we do a quick interview. Approaching the finish line, the lights are blindingly bright, and the music is loudly thump-thumping away. I am shocked at how many people are still around. Thirty feet from the finish, the Race Director comes out to greet Jon and accompany him in. The shutters of a dozen cameras snap away. It is a glorious sight, and the several dozen people still there cheer wildly. Jon comes alive and dramatically strides across the finish line. He basks in the congratulatory glow of his historic just-completed marathon. His unofficial time is eleven hours and twenty-three minutes, and at ninety-six years old, he is the oldest person to ever complete the New York City Marathon.

He is immediately escorted to the medical tent as a precaution. Once there, resting comfortably on a cot, Jon pulls out three small bottles of Johnnie Walker Black scotch from his coat pocket. Unbeknownst to us, he carried them the entire distance. He flashes a brilliant smile as we each take one, unscrew the caps, and enthusiastically toast Jon's record-setting day. "Twenty-six at ninety-six!"

Afterword

This book is dedicated to my life partner, Kate Berman.

In April of 2020, at the age of sixty-one, Kate suffered cardiac arrest. It was sudden and unexpected; she did not survive. She exercised regularly, ate healthily, and had no known history of heart problems. In the prior two decades, she completed a dozen marathons and a multiday team triathlon event.

Beloved partner. Super Mom. Dedicated daughter. Loyal friend. Unselfish to a fault, always attending to others' needs before her own. Kind, solicitous, strong, compassionate, courageous, humble, and gracious. High energy with a powerful and infectious can-do spirit. Servant community leader possessing a big, charitable heart.

Kate had a bumper sticker on her bookcase, a gift from a friend, which said, "Ultimate Mom." That, more than anything, was Kate. She always put family first, subordinating her own considerable career ambitions to focus on raising our children and supporting me. She was our family's heart and soul.

My draft manuscript was already completed when we lost her. As I created this narrative, Kate was my number-one reader and critic. She helped to keep my memory fresh, my voice authentic, and my descriptions accurate.

Kate and I shared forty years together, both of us giving and receiving. Truth be told, Kate always gave more than she got. That is true of our marriage, as well as with so many of her relationships.

That was Kate, perpetual giver. And she never complained; she just kept on giving.

She supported me through successes and failures, through the rollercoaster of multiple transitions. I would not have a story to tell if it wasn't for Kate. I would not have made the same choices if it wasn't for Kate. I would not be who I am if it wasn't for Kate. Her influence was life-changing, and her support was unflinching. She is lovingly and gratefully remembered.

And to our three children—Max, Elena, and Elizabeth—you, too, made this story possible, both in the living and the telling. You inspired me in so many ways. You still do, more than ever. You carry your mother's light. Through you it shines brightly in this world. With every new day, that light adds enriching detail, depth, and texture to our family's story. You make the world a better place, and I could not be prouder of you.

Acknowledgments

I am very fortunate; I was supported, encouraged, guided, and inspired by so many others.

Thank you to Nicole Helget, my writing instructor at the Loft Literary Center, for her compassion, insights, and encouragement early on. At a time when I had major doubts, she helped me to believe that I could do this. And thank you to my entire class of aspiring authors, whose critical feedback was often painful to hear but always insightful, helpful, and gratefully received.

Thank you to Laurie Herrmann and the entire team at Beaver's Pond Press for giving me the opportunity to tell my story. I extend a special thanks to my editor, Kerry Stapley. I received advice early on to find an editor who "gets me," and in Kerry I thankfully did. Kerry's incisive criticism and enthusiastic encouragement were offered in abundant quantities. My work always got better after hearing from her. She was the best imaginable partner.

Thank you to friends Barb and Helen, who read earlier drafts and provided insightful perspectives and encouragement that kept me moving forward.

Thank you to friends and former American Express colleagues, Cherie and Kris, for helping me to keep the corporate chapters thoughtful, honest, and real.

Thank you to my friend, Dawn, who encouraged me from start to finish—with creative advice, critical feedback, and inspiration from her own experience as a highly successful author.

My most heartfelt thanks—for sheer inspiration and the love and support they always provided—goes to my entire family. Mom, Dad, and Kate are my lifetime role models. They helped to form my core and will always be in in my heart. Thank you to my siblings, Henry and Laura, for being patient readers, very kind supporters, and helpful in jogging long-distant memories. And thank you to my children, Max, Elena, and Elizabeth, for always encouraging and inspiring me. My greatest hope is to make you proud .

CREDITS

Lyrics from "Who Will Buy?" are from Oliver by Lionel Bart, © TRO/ Essex Music Group. (Lyrics as quoted herein were added to the stage and movie versions of *Oliver* but are not part of the song licensed by TRO/Essex Music Group.)

Lines from "Transit" are from *Playlist for the Apocalypse* by Rita Dove (W. W. Norton, New York, 2021) and are reprinted by permission of Ms. Dove.

Excerpt from *Kafka on the Shore* is by Haruki Murakami, translated by Philip Gabriel, translation © 2005 by Haruki Murakami, and reprinted by permission from Alfred A. Knopf, a division of Penguin Random House LLC.

Lyrics from "I Can't Give You Anything but Love," words and music by Jimmy McHugh and Dorothy Fields, © 1928 Cotton Club Publishing and administered by Sony Music Publishing (US) LLC, 424 Church Street, Suite 1200, Nashville, TN 37219; and Shapiro, Bernstein & Co., Inc., and administered by Reservoir Media Management, Inc. Reprinted by permission of Hal Leonard.

Lyrics from "Night and Day," words and music by Cole Porter, © 1932 (Renewed) WB Music Corp., are reprinted by permission from Alfred Music.

Lines from the poem "There Comes the Strangest Moment" by Kate Light are from *Open Slowly* (Zoo Press, 2003).

Excerpt from *What I Talk About When I Talk About Running* is by Haruki Murakami, translated by Philip Gabriel, translation © 2008 by Haruki Murakami, and reprinted by permission of Alfred A. Knopf, an imprint of the Knopf Doubleday Publishing Group, a division of Penguin Random House LLC.